Adventures in the
Rocky Mountains

Deep in the heart of the Rocky Mountains, 1873

ISABELLA BIRD

Adventures in the Rocky Mountains

GREAT
JOURNEYS

PENGUIN BOOKS

Published by the Penguin Group
Penguin Books Ltd, 80 Strand, London WC2R 0RL, England
Penguin Group (USA) Inc., 375 Hudson Street, New York, New York 10014, USA
Penguin Group (Canada), 90 Eglinton Avenue East, Suite 700, Toronto, Ontario, Canada M4P 2Y3
(a division of Pearson Penguin Canada Inc.)
Penguin Ireland, 25 St Stephen's Green, Dublin 2, Ireland (a division of Penguin Books Ltd)
Penguin Group (Australia), 250 Camberwell Road, Camberwell, Victoria 3124, Australia
(a division of Pearson Australia Group Pty Ltd)
Penguin Books India Pvt Ltd, 11 Community Centre, Panchsheel Park, New Delhi – 110 017, India
Penguin Group (NZ), 67 Apollo Drive, Rosedale, North Shore 0632, New Zealand
(a division of Pearson New Zealand Ltd)
Penguin Books (South Africa) (Pty) Ltd, 24 Sturdee Avenue, Rosebank, Johannesburg 2196, South Africa

Penguin Books Ltd, Registered Offices: 80 Strand, London WC2R 0RL, England

www.penguin.com

A Lady's Life in the Rocky Mountains first published 1879
This extract first published in Penguin Books 2007
1

Inside-cover maps by Jeff Edwards

Typeset by Rowland Phototypesetting Ltd, Bury St Edmunds, Suffolk
Printed in England by Clays Ltd, St Ives plc

ISBN: 978-0-141-03209-2

Isabella Lucy Bird (1831–1904) was the daughter of a clergyman and grew up in Tattenhall, Cheshire. Early in life she suffered from a spinal complaint and in 1854 she was sent by her doctor to America and Canada to improve her health. She continued to suffer from back trouble, depression and insomnia until, at the age of forty, she set off for Australia and Hawaii where her health miraculously improved and she climbed the world's largest volcano. In 1873, Isabella Bird set off for the Rocky Mountains. At that time, Colorado, where she stayed longest, was an untamed territory outside the Union, its virgin lands inhabited by hard-living, hard-drinking pioneer settlers who had only recently and brutally seized them from the Indians. Isabella's intrepid journeys within this fantastic landscape are relayed in the form of vivid letters she wrote to her adored sister, Henrietta.

Letter I

Lake Tahoe, September 2

I have found a dream of beauty at which one might look all one's life and sigh. Not lovable, like the Sandwich Islands,[1] but beautiful in its own way! A strictly North American beauty – snow-splotched mountains, huge pines, red-woods, sugar pines, silver spruce; a crystalline atmosphere, waves of the richest colour; and a pine-hung lake which mirrors all beauty on its surface. Lake Tahoe is before me, a sheet of water twenty-two miles long by ten broad, and in some places 1700 feet deep. It lies at a height of 6000 feet, and the snow-crowned summits which wall it in are from 8000 to 11,000 feet in altitude. The air is keen and elastic. There is no sound but the distant and slightly musical ring of the lumberer's axe.

It is a weariness to go back, even in thought, to the clang of San Francisco, which I left in its cold morning fog early yesterday, driving to the Oakland ferry through streets with side-walks heaped with thousands of cantaloupe and water-melons, tomatoes, cucumbers, squashes, pears, grapes, peaches, apricots, – all of startling size as compared with any I ever saw before. Other

[1] Hawaii

streets were piled with sacks of flour, left out all night, owing to the security from rain at this season. I pass hastily over the early part of the journey, the crossing the bay in a fog as chill as November, the number of 'lunch baskets,' which gave the car the look of conveying a great picnic party, the last view of the Pacific, on which I had looked for nearly a year, the fierce sunshine and brilliant sky inland, the look of long *rainlessness*, which one may not call drought, the valleys with sides crimson with the poison oak, the dusty vineyards, with great purple clusters thick among the leaves, and between the vines great dusty melons lying on the dusty earth. From off the boundless harvest-fields the grain was carried in June, and it is now stacked in sacks along the track, awaiting freightage. California is a 'land flowing with milk and honey.' The barns are bursting with fullness. In the dusty orchards the apple and pear branches are supported, that they may not break down under the weight of fruit; melons, tomatoes, and squashes of gigantic size lie almost unheeded on the ground; fat cattle, gorged almost to repletion shade themselves under the oaks; superb 'red' horses shine, not with grooming, but with condition; and thriving farms everywhere show on what a solid basis the prosperity of the 'Golden State' is founded. Very uninviting, however rich, was the blazing Sacramento Valley, and very repulsive the city of Sacramento, which, at a distance of 125 miles from the Pacific, has an elevation of only thirty feet. The mercury stood at 103° in the shade, and the fine white dust was stifling.

In the late afternoon we began the ascent of the

Sierras, whose saw-like points had been in sight for many miles. The dusty fertility was all left behind, the country became rocky and gravelly, and deeply scored by streams bearing the muddy wash of the mountain gold-mines down to the muddier Sacramento. There were long broken ridges and deep ravines, the ridges becoming longer, the ravines deeper, the pines thicker and larger, as we ascended into a cool atmosphere of exquisite purity, and before six P.M. the last traces of cultivation and the last hardwood trees were left behind.

At Colfax, a station at a height of 2400 feet, I got out and walked the length of the train. First came two great gaudy engines, the Grizzly Bear and the White Fox, with their respective tenders loaded with logs of wood, the engines with great, solitary, reflecting lamps in front above the cow-guards, a quantity of polished brass-work, comfortable glass houses, and well-stuffed seats for the engine-drivers. The engines and tenders were succeeded by a baggage-car, a mail-car, and Wells, Fargo, and Co.'s express-car, the latter loaded with bullion and valuable parcels, and in charge of two 'express agents.' Each of these cars is forty-five feet long. Then came two cars loaded with peaches and grapes; then two 'silver palace' cars, each sixty feet long; then a smoking-car, at that time occupied mainly by Chinamen; and then five ordinary passenger-cars, with platforms like all the others, making altogether a train about 700 feet in length. The platforms of the four front cars were clustered over with Digger Indians, with their squaws, children, and gear. They are perfect savages, without any aptitude for even aboriginal civilisation, and are altogether the most degraded of the ill-fated tribes which are dying out before the white races. They were all very diminutive, five feet one inch being, I should think, about the average height, with flat noses, wide mouths, and black hair, cut straight above the eyes and hanging lank and long at the back and sides. The squaws wore their hair thickly plastered with pitch, and a broad band of the same across their noses and cheeks. They carried their infants on their backs, strapped to boards. The clothing of both sexes was a ragged, dirty combination of coarse woollen cloth and hide, the moccasins being unornamented. They were all hideous and filthy, and swarming with vermin. The men carried short bows and arrows, one of them, who appeared to be the chief, having a lynx's skin for a quiver. A few had fishing-tackle, but the bystanders said that they lived almost entirely upon grasshoppers. They were a most impressive incongruity in the midst of the tokens of an omnipotent civilisation.

The light of the sinking sun from that time glorified the Sierras, and as the dew fell, aromatic odours made the still air sweet. On a single track, sometimes carried on a narrow ledge excavated from the mountain side by men lowered from the top in baskets, overhanging ravines from 2000 to 3000 feet deep, the monster train *snaked* its way upwards, stopping sometimes in front of a few frame houses, at others where nothing was to be seen but a log cabin with a few Chinamen hanging about it, but where trails on the sides of the ravines pointed to a gold country above and below. So sharp and frequent are the curves on some parts of the ascent, that on looking out of the window one could seldom see more than a part of the train at once. At Cape Horn, where the track curves round the ledge of a precipice 2500 feet in depth, it is correct to be frightened, and a fashion of holding the breath and shutting the eyes prevails, but my fears were reserved for the crossing of a trestle-bridge over a very deep chasm, which is itself approached by a sharp curve. This bridge appeared to be overlapped by the cars so as to produce the effect of looking down directly into a wild gulch, with a torrent raging along it at an immense depth below.

Shivering in the keen, frosty air near the summit-pass of the Sierras, we entered the 'snow-sheds,' wooden galleries, which for about fifty miles shut out all the splendid views of the region, as given in dioramas, not even allowing a glimpse of 'the Gem of the Sierras,' the lovely Donner Lake. One of these sheds is twenty-seven miles long. In a few hours the mercury had fallen from 103° to 29°, and we had ascended 6987 feet in 105 miles! After passing through the sheds, we had several grand views of a pine-forest on fire before reaching Truckee at 11 P.M., having travelled 258 miles. Truckee, the centre of the 'lumbering region' of the Sierras, is usually spoken of as 'a rough mountain town,' and Mr W. had told me that all the roughs of the district congregated there, that there were nightly pistol affrays in bar-rooms, etc., but as he admitted that a lady was sure of respect, and Mr G. strongly advised me to stay and see the lakes, I got out, much dazed, and very stupid with sleep, envying the people in the sleeping-car, who were already unconscious on their luxurious couches. The cars drew up in a street – if street that could be called which was only a wide, cleared space, intersected by rails, with here and there a stump, and great piles of sawn logs bulking big in the moonlight, and a number of irregular clap-board, steep-roofed houses, many of them with open fronts, glaring with light and crowded with men. We had pulled up at the door of a rough Western hotel, with a partially open front, being a bar-room crowded with men drinking and smoking, and the space between it and the cars was a moving mass of loafers and passengers. On the tracks, engines, tolling heavy bells, were mightily moving, the glare from their cyclopean eyes dulling the light of a forest which was burning fitfully on a mountain side; and on open spaces great fires of pine-logs were burning cheerily, with groups of men round them. A band was playing noisily, and the unholy sound of tom-toms was not far off. Mountains – the sierras of many a fireside dream – seemed to wall in the town, and great pines stood out, sharp and clear cut, against a sky in which a moon and stars were shining frostily.

It was a sharp frost at that great height, and when an 'irrepressible nigger,' who seemed to represent the hotel establishment, deposited me and my carpet-bag in a room which answered for 'the parlour,' I was glad to find some remains of pine knots still alight in the stove. A man came in and said that when the cars were gone he would try to get me a room, but they were so full that it would be a very poor one. The crowd was solely masculine. It was then 11.30 P.M., and I had not had a meal since 6 A.M.; but when I asked hopefully for a hot supper, with tea, I was told that no supper could be got at that hour; but in half an hour the same man returned with a small cup of cold, weak tea, and a small slice of bread, which looked as if it had been much handled.

I asked the negro factotum about the hire of horses, and presently a man came in from the bar who, he said, could supply my needs. This man, the very type of a western pioneer, bowed, threw himself into a rocking-chair, drew a spittoon beside him, cut a fresh quid of tobacco, began to chew energetically, and put his feet, cased in miry high boots, into which his trousers were tucked, on the top of the stove. He said he had horses which would both 'lope' and trot, that some ladies preferred the Mexican saddle, that I could ride alone in perfect safety; and after a route had been devised, I hired a horse for two days. This man wore a pioneer's badge as one of the earliest settlers of California, but he had moved on as one place after another had become too civilised for him, 'but nothing,' he added, 'was likely to change much in Truckee.' I was afterwards told that the usual regular hours of sleep are not observed there. The accommodation is too limited for the population of 2000, which is masculine mainly, and is liable to frequent temporary additions, and beds are occupied continuously, though by different occupants, throughout the greater part of the twenty-four hours. Consequently I found the bed and room allotted to me quite tumbled-looking. Men's coats and sticks were hanging up, miry boots were littered about, and a rifle was in one corner. There was no window to the outer air, but I slept soundly, being only once awoke by an increase of the same din in which I had fallen asleep, varied by three pistol-shots fired in rapid succession.

This morning Truckee wore a totally different aspect. The crowds of the night before had disappeared. There were heaps of ashes where the fires had been. A sleepy German waiter seemed the only person about the premises, the open drinking-saloons were nearly empty, and only a few sleepy-looking loafers hung about in what is called the street. It might have been Sunday; but they say that it brings a great accession of throng and jollity. Public worship has died out at present; work is discontinued on Sunday, but the day is given up to pleasure. Putting a minimum of indispensables into a bag, and slipping on my Hawaiian riding-dress over a silk skirt, and a dust-cloak over all, I stealthily crossed the *plaza* to the livery-stable, the largest building in Truckee, where twelve fine horses were stabled in stalls on each side of a broad drive. My friend of the evening before showed me his 'rig,' three velvet-covered side-saddles almost without horns. Some ladies, he said, used the horn of the Mexican saddle, but none 'in this part' rode cavalier fashion. I felt abashed. I could not ride any distance in the conventional mode, and was just going to give up this splendid 'ravage,' when the man said, 'Ride your own fashion; here, at Truckee, if anywhere in the world, people can do as they like.' Blissful Truckee! In no time a large grey horse was 'rigged out' in a handsome silver-bossed Mexican saddle, with ornamental leather tassels hanging from the stirrup-guards, and a housing of black bear's-skin. I strapped my silk skirt on the saddle, deposited my cloak in the corn-bin, and was safely on the horse's back before his owner had time to devise any way of mounting me. Neither he nor any of the loafers who had assembled showed the slightest sign of astonishment, but all were as respectful as possible.

Once on horseback my embarrassment disappeared, and I rode through Truckee, whose irregular, steep-roofed house and shanties, set down in a clearing, and surrounded closely by mountain and forest, looked like a temporary encampment, passed under the Pacific Railroad, and then for twelve miles followed the windings of the Truckee river, a clear, rushing, mountain stream, in which immense pine logs had gone aground not to be floated off till the next freshet, a loud-tongued, rollicking stream of ice-cold water, on whose banks no ferns or trailers hang, and which leaves no greeness along its turbulent progress. All was bright with that brilliancy of sky and atmosphere, that blaze of sunshine and universal glitter, which I never saw till I came to California, combined with an elasticity in the air which removes all lassitude, and gives one spirit enough for anything. On either side of the Truckee great sierras rose like walls, castellated, embattled, rifted, skirted and crowned with pines of enormous size, the walls now and then breaking apart to show some snow-slashed peak rising into a heaven of intense, unclouded, sunny blue. At this altitude of 6000 feet one must learn to be content with varieties of *coniferece*, for, except for aspens, which spring up in some places where the pines have been cleared away, and for cottonwoods, which at a lower level fringe the streams, there is nothing but the bear cherry, the raspberry, the gooseberry, the wild grape, and the wild currant. None of these grew near the Truckee, but I feasted my eyes on pines which, though not so large as the Wellingtonia of the Yosemite, are really gigantic, attaining a height of 250 feet, their huge stems, the warm red of cedar wood, rising straight and branchless for a third of their height, their diameter from seven to fifteen feet, their shape that of a larch, but with the needles long and dark, and cones a foot long. Pines cleft the sky; they were massed wherever level ground occurred; they stood over the Truckee at right angles, or lay across it in prostrate grandeur. Their stumps and carcasses were everywhere; and smooth 'shoots' on the sierras marked where they were shot down as 'felled timber,' to be floated off by the river. To them this wild region owes its scattered population, and the sharp ring of the lumberer's axe mingles with the cries of wild beasts and the roar of mountain torrents.

The track is a soft, natural, waggon road, very pleasant to ride on. The horse was much too big for me, and had plans of his own; but now and then, where the ground admitted of it, I tried his heavy 'lope' with much amusement. I met nobody, and passed nothing on the road but a freight waggon, drawn by twenty-two oxen, guided by three fine-looking young men, who had some difficulty in making room for me to pass their awkward convoy. After I had ridden about ten miles the road went up a steep hill in the forest, turned abruptly, and through the blue gloom of the great pines which rose from the ravine in which the river was then hid, came glimpses of two mountains, about 11,000 feet in height, whose bald grey summits were crowned with pure snow. It was one of those glorious surprises in scenery which make one feel as if one must bow down and worship. The forest was thick, and had an undergrowth of dwarf spruce and brambles, but as the horse had become fidgety and 'scary' on the track, I turned off in the idea of taking a short cut, and was sitting carelessly, shortening my stirrup, when a great, dark, hairy beast rose, crashing and snorting, out of the tangle just in front of me. I had only a glimpse of him, and thought that my imagination had magnified a wild boar, but it was a bear. The horse snorted and plunged violently, as if he would go down to the river, and then turned, still plunging, up a steep bank, when, finding that I must come off, I threw myself off on the right side, where the ground rose considerably, so that I had not far to fall. I got up covered with dust, but neither shaken nor bruised. It was truly grotesque and humiliating. The bear ran in one direction, and the horse in another. I hurried after the latter, and twice he stopped till I was close to him, then turned round and cantered away. After walking about a mile in deep dust, I picked up first the saddle-blanket and next my bag, and soon came upon the horse, standing facing me, and shaking all over. I thought I should catch him then, but when I went up to him he turned round, threw up his heels several times, rushed off the track, galloped in circles, bucking, kicking, and plunging for some time, and then throwing up his heels as an act of final defiance, went off at full speed in the direction of Truckee, with the saddle over his shoulders and the great wooden stirrups thumping his sides, while I trudged ignominiously along in the dust, laboriously carrying the bag and saddle-blanket.

I walked for nearly an hour, heated and hungry, when to my joy I saw the ox-team halted across the top of a gorge, and one of the teamsters leading the horse towards me. The young man said that, seeing the horse coming, they had drawn the team across the road to stop him, and remembering that he had passed them with a lady on him, they feared that there had been an accident, and had just saddled one of their own horses to go in search of me. He brought me some water to wash the dust from my face, and re-saddled the horse, but the animal snorted and plunged for some time before he would let me mount, and then sidled along in such a nervous and scared way, that the teamster walked for some distance by me to see that I was 'all right.' He said that the woods in the neighbourhood of Tahoe had been full of brown and grizzly bears for some days, but that no one was in any danger from them. I took a long gallop beyond the scene of my tumble to quiet the horse, who was most restless and troublesome.

Then the scenery became truly magnificent and

bright with life. Crested blue-jays darted through the dark pines, squirrels in hundreds scampered through the forest, red dragon-flies flashed like 'living light,' exquisite chipmonks ran across the track, but only a dusty blue lupin here and there reminded me of earth's fairer children. Then the river became broad and still, and mirrored in its transparent depths regal pines, straight as an arrow, with rich yellow and green lichen clinging to their stems, and firs and balsam-pines filling up the spaces between them, the gorge opened, and this mountain-girdled lake lay before me, with its margin broken up into bays and promontories, most picturesquely clothed by huge sugar-pines. It lay dimpling and scintillating beneath the noonday sun, as entirely unspoilt as fifteen years ago, when its pure loveliness was known only to trappers and Indians. One man lives on it the whole year round; otherwise early October strips its shores of their few inhabitants, and thereafter, for seven months, it is rarely accessible except on snow-shoes. It never freezes. In the dense forests which bound it, and drape two-thirds of its gaunt sierras, are hordes of grizzlies, brown bears, wolves, elk, deer, chipmonks, martens, minks, skunks, foxes, squirrels, and snakes. On its margin I found an irregular wooden inn, with a lumber-waggon at the door, on which was the carcass of a large grizzly bear, shot behind the house this morning. I had intended to ride ten miles farther, but finding that the trail in some places was a 'blind' one, and being bewitched by the beauty and serenity of Tahoe, I have remained here sketching, revelling in the view from the verandah, and strolling in the forest. At this height there is frost every night of the year, and my fingers are benumbed.

The beauty is entrancing. The sinking sun is out of sight behind the western sierras, and all the pine-hung promontories on the side of the water are rich indigo, just reddened with lake, deepening here and there into Tyrian purple. The peaks above, which still catch the sun, are bright rose-red, and all the mountains on the other side are pink; and pink, too, are the far-off summits on which the snow-drifts rest. Indigo, red, and orange tints stain the still water, which lies solemn and dark against the shore, under the shadow of stately pines. An hour later, and a moon nearly full – not a pale, flat disc, but a radiant sphere – has wheeled up into the flushed sky. The sunset has passed through every stage of beauty, through every glory of colour, through riot and triumph, through pathos and tenderness, into a long, dreamy, painless rest, succeeded by the profound solemnity of the moonlight, and a stillness broken only by the night cries of beasts in the aromatic forests.

Letter II

Cheyenne, Wyoming, September 7

I dreamt of bears so vividly that I woke with a furry death-hug at my throat, but feeling quite refreshed. When I mounted my horse after breakfast the sun was high and the air so keen and intoxicating that, giving the animal his head, I galloped up and down hill, feeling completely tireless. Truly, that air is the elixir of life. I had a glorious ride back to Truckee. The road was not as solitary as the day before. In a deep part of the forest the horse snorted and reared, and I saw a cinnamon-coloured bear with two cubs cross the track ahead of me. I tried to keep the horse quiet that the mother might acquit me of any designs upon her lolloping children, but I was glad when the ungainly, long-haired party crossed the river. Then I met a team, the driver of which stopped and said he was glad that I had not gone to Cornelian Bay, it was such a bad trail, and hoped I had enjoyed Tahoe. The driver of another team stopped and asked if I had seen any bears. Then a man heavily armed, a hunter probably, asked me if I were the English tourist who had 'happened on' a 'grizzlie' yesterday. Then I saw a lumberer taking his dinner on a rock in the river, who 'touched his hat' and brought me a draught of ice-cold water, which

I could hardly drink owing to the fractiousness of the horse, and gathered me some mountain pinks, which I admired. I mention these little incidents to indicate the habit of respectful courtesy to women which prevails in that region. These men might have been excused for speaking in a somewhat free-and-easy tone to a lady riding alone, and in an unwonted fashion. Womanly dignity and manly respect for women are the salt of society in this wild West.

My horse was so excitable that I avoided the centre of Truckee, and skulked through a collection of Chinamen's shanties to the stable, where a prodigious roan horse, standing seventeen hands high, was produced for my ride to the Donner Lake. I asked the owner, who was as interested in my enjoying myself as a West Highlander might have been, if there were not ruffians about who might make an evening ride dangerous. A story was current of a man having ridden through Truckee two evenings before with a chopped-up human body in a sack behind the saddle, and hosts of stories of ruffianism are located there, rightly or wrongly. This man said, 'There's a bad breed of ruffians, but the ugliest among them all won't touch you. There's nothing Western folk admire so much as pluck in a woman.' I had to get on a barrel before I could reach the stirrup, and when I was mounted my feet only came half-way down the horse's sides. I felt like a fly on him. The road at first lay through a valley without a river, but some swampishness nourished some rank swamp-grass, the first *green* grass I have seen in America; and the pines, with their red stems, looked beautiful rising out of it. I hurried along, and came upon the Donner Lake quite suddenly, to be completely smitten by its beauty. It is only about three miles long by one and a half broad, and lies hidden away among mountains, with no dwellings on its shores but some deserted lumberers' cabins. Its loneliness pleased me well. I did not see man, beast, or bird from the time I left Truckee till I returned. The mountains, which rise abruptly from the margin, are covered with dense pine-forests, through which, here and there, strange forms of bare grey rock, castellated, or needle-like, protrude themselves. On the opposite side, at a height of about 6000 feet, a grey, ascending line, from which rumbling, incoherent sounds occasionally proceeded, is seen through the pines. This is one of the snow-sheds of the Pacific Railroad, which shuts out from travellers all that I was seeing. The lake is called after Mr Donner, who, with his family, arrived at the Truckee river in the fall of the year, in company with a party of emigrants bound for California. Being encumbered with many cattle, he let the company pass on, and, with his own party of sixteen souls, which included his wife and four children, encamped by the lake. In the morning they found themselves surrounded by an expanse of snow, and after some consultation it was agreed that the whole party except Mr Donner, who was unwell, his wife, and a German friend, should take the horses and attempt to cross the mountain, which, after much peril, they succeeded in doing; but, as the storm continued for several weeks, it was impossible for any rescue party to succour the three who had been left behind. In the early spring, when the snow was hard enough for travelling, a party started in quest, expecting to find the snow-bound alive and well, as they had cattle enough for their support, and, after weeks of toil and exposure, they scaled the Sierras and reached the Donner Lake. On arriving at the camp they opened the rude door, and there, sitting before the fire, they found the German, holding a roasted human arm and hand, which he was greedily eating. The rescue party overpowered him, and with difficulty tore the arm from him. A short search discovered the body of the lady, minus the arm, frozen in the snow, round, plump, and fair, showing that she was in perfect health when she met her fate. The rescuers returned to California, taking the German with them, whose story was that Mr Donner died in the fall, and that the cattle escaped, leaving them but little food, and that when this was exhausted Mrs Donner died. The story never gained any credence, and the truth oozed out that the German had murdered the husband, then brutally murdered the wife, and had seized upon Donner's money. There were, however, no witnesses, and the murderer escaped with the enforced surrender of the money to the Donner orphans.

This tragic story filled my mind as I rode towards the head of the lake, which became every moment grander and more unutterably lovely. The sun was setting fast, and against his golden light green promontories, wooded with stately pines, stood out one beyond another in a medium of dark rich blue, while grey bleached summits, peaked, turreted, and snow-slashed, were piled above them, gleaming with amber light. Darker grew the blue gloom, the dew fell heavily, aromatic odours floated on the air, and still the lofty peaks glowed with living light, till in one second it died off from them, leaving them with the ashy paleness of a dead face. It was dark and cold under the mountain shadows, the frosty chill of the high altitude wrapped me round, the solitude was overwhelming, and I reluctantly turned my horse's head towards Truckee, often looking back to the ashy summits in their unearthly fascination. Eastwards the look of the scenery was changing every moment, while the lake for long remained 'one burnished sheet of living gold,' and Truckee lay utterly out of sight in a hollow filled with lake and cobalt. Before long a carnival of colour began which I can only describe as delirious, intoxicating, a hardly bearable joy, a tender anguish, an indescribable yearning, an unearthly music, rich in love and worship. It lasted considerably more than an hour, and though the road was growing very dark, and the train which was to take me thence was fast climbing the Sierras, I could not ride faster than a walk.

The eastward mountains, which had been grey, blushed pale pink, the pink deepened into rose, and the rose into crimson, and then all solidity etherealised away and became clear and pure as an amethyst, while all the waving ranges and the broken pine-clothed ridges below etherealised too, but into a dark rich blue, and a strange effect of atmosphere blended the whole into one perfect picture. It changed, deepened, reddened, melted, growing more and more wonderful, while under the pines it was night, till, having displayed itself for an hour, the jewelled peaks suddenly became like those of the sierras, wan as the face of death. Far later the cold golden light lingered in the west, with pines in relief against its purity, and where the rose light had glowed in the east, a huge moon upheaved itself, and the red flicker of forest fires luridly streaked the mountain sides near and far off. I realised that night had come with its *eeriness*, and putting my great horse into a gallop I clung on to him till I pulled him up in Truckee, which was at the height of its evening revelries – fires blazing out of doors, bar-rooms and saloons crammed, lights glaring, gaming-tables thronged, fiddle and banjo in frightful discord, and the air ringing with ribaldry and profanity.

Letter III

Cheyenne, Wyoming, September 8

Cheyenne is described as 'a God-forsaken, God-forgotten place.' That it forgets God is written on its face. It owes its existence to the railroad, and has diminished in population, but is a depôt for a large amount of the necessaries of life which are distributed through the scantily settled districts within distances of 300 miles by 'freight waggons,' each drawn by four or six horses or mules, or double that number of oxen. At times over 100 waggons, with double that number of teamsters, are in Cheyenne at once. A short time ago it was a perfect pandemonium, mainly inhabited by rowdies and desperadoes, the scum of advancing civilisation; and murders, stabbings, shootings, and pistol affrays were at times events of almost hourly occurrence in its drinking dens. But in the West, when things reach their worst, a sharp and sure remedy is provided. Those settlers who find the state of matters intolerable, organise themselves into a Vigilance Committee. 'Judge Lynch,' with a few feet of rope, appears on the scene, the majority crystallises round the supporters of order, warnings are issued to obnoxious people, simply bearing a scrawl of a tree with a man dangling from it, with such words as 'Clear out of this by 6 A.M., or –.' A number of the worst desperadoes are tried by a yet more summary process than a drumhead court-martial, 'strung up,' and buried ignominiously. I have been told that 120 ruffians were disposed of in this way here in a single fortnight. Cheyenne is now as safe as Hilo, and the interval between the most desperate lawlessness and the time when United States law, with its corruption and feebleness, comes upon the scene is one of comparative security and good order. Piety is not the *forte* of Cheyenne. The roads resound with atrocious profanity, and the rowdyism of the saloons and bar-rooms is repressed, not extirpated.

[. . .]

Fort Collins, September 10

It gave me a strange sensation to embark upon the Plains. Plains, plains everywhere, plains generally level, but elsewhere rolling in long undulations, like the waves of a sea which had fallen asleep. They are covered thinly with buff grass, the withered stalks of flowers, Spanish bayonet, and a small beehive-shaped cactus. One could gallop all over them.

They are peopled with large villages of what are called prairie dogs, because they utter a short, sharp bark, but the dogs are, in reality, marmots. We passed numbers of these villages, which are composed of raised circular orifices, about eighteen inches in diameter, with sloping passages leading downwards for five or six feet. Hundreds of these burrows are placed together. On nearly every rim a small furry reddish-buff beast sat on his hind legs, looking, so far as head went, much like a young seal. These creatures were acting as sentinels, and sunning themselves. As we passed, each gave a warning yelp, shook its tail, and, with a ludicrous flourish of its hind legs, dived into its hole. The appearance of hundreds of these creatures, each eighteen inches long, sitting like dogs begging, with their paws down and all turned sunwards, is most grotesque. The Wish-ton-Wish has few enemies, and is a most prolific animal. From its enormous increase, and the energy and extent of its burrowing operations, one can fancy that in the course of years the prairies will be seriously injured, as it honeycombs the ground, and renders it unsafe for horses. The burrows seem usually to be shared by owls, and many of the people insist that a rattlesnake is also an inmate, but I hope, for the sake of the harmless, cheery little prairie dog, that this unwelcome fellowship is a myth.

[. . .]

It is the election day for the Territory, and men were galloping over the prairie to register their votes. The three in the waggon talked politics the whole time. They spoke openly and shamelessly of the prices given for votes; and apparently there was not a politician on either side who was not accused of degrading corruption. We saw a convoy of 5000 head of Texan cattle travelling from Southern Texas to Iowa. They had been nine months on the way! They were under the charge of twenty mounted *vacheros*, heavily armed, and a light waggon accompanied them, full of extra rifles and ammunition, not unnecessary, for the Indians are raiding in all directions, maddened by the reckless and useless slaughter of the buffalo, which is their chief subsistence. On the plains are herds of wild horses, buffalo, deer, and antelope; and in the mountains, bears, wolves, deer, elk, mountain lions, bison, and mountain sheep. You see a rifle in every waggon, as people always hope to fall in with game.

By the time we reached Fort Collins I was sick and dizzy with the heat of the sun, and not disposed to be pleased with a most unpleasing place. It was a military post, but at present consists of a few frame houses put down recently on the bare and burning plain. The settlers have 'great expectations,' but of what? The mountains look hardly nearer than from Greeley; one only realises their vicinity by the loss of their higher peaks. This house is freer from bugs than the one at Greeley, but full of flies. These new settlements are altogether revolting, entirely utilitarian, given up to talk of dollars as well as to making them, with coarse speech, coarse food, coarse everything, nothing wherewith to satisfy the higher cravings if they exist, nothing on which the eye can rest with pleasure. The lower floor of this inn swarms with locusts in addition to thousands of black flies. The latter cover the ground and rise buzzing from it as you walk.

Letter IV

Canyon, September 12

I was actually so dull and tired that I deliberately slept away the afternoon in order to forget the heat and flies. Thirty men in working clothes, silent and sad-looking, came in to supper. The beef was tough and greasy, the butter had turned to oil, and beef and butter were black with living, drowned, and half-drowned flies. The greasy table-cloth was black also with flies, and I did not wonder that the guests looked melancholy and quickly escaped. I failed to get a horse, but was strongly recommended to come here and board with a settler, who, they said, had a saw-mill and took boarders. The person who recommended it so strongly gave me a note of introduction, and told me that it was in a grand part of the mountains, where many people had been camping out all the summer for the benefit of their health. The idea of a boarding-house, as I know them in America, was rather formidable in the present state of my wardrobe, and I decided on bringing my carpet-bag, as well as my pack, lest I should be rejected for my bad clothes. Early the next morning I left in a buggy drawn by light *broncos* and driven by a profoundly melancholy young man. He had never been to the canyon; there was no road. We met nobody, saw nothing except antelope in the distance, and he became more melancholy and lost his way, driving hither and thither for about twenty miles till we came upon an old trail which eventually brought us to a fertile 'bottom,' where hay and barley were being harvested, and five or six frame houses looked cheerful. I had been recommended to two of these, which professed to take in strangers, but one was full of reapers, and in the other a child was dead. So I took the buggy on, glad to leave the glaring, prosaic settlement behind. There was a most curious loneliness about the journey up to that time. Except for the huge barrier to the right, the boundless prairies were everywhere, and it was like being at sea without a compass. The wheels made neither sound nor indentation as we drove over the short, dry grass, and there was no cheerful clatter of horses' hoofs. The sky was cloudy and the air hot and still. In one place we passed the carcass of a mule, and a number of vultures soared up from it, to descend again immediately. Skeletons and bones of animals were often to be seen. A range of low, grassy hills, called the Foot Hills, rose from the plain, featureless and monotonous, except where streams, fed by the snows of the higher regions, had cut their way through them. Confessedly bewildered, and more melancholy than ever, the driver turned up one of the widest of these entrances, and in another hour the Foot Hills lay between us and the prairie sea, and a higher and broken range, with pitch pines of average size, was revealed behind them. These Foot Hills, which swell up uninterestingly from the plains on their eastern side, on their western have the appearance of having broken off from the next range, and the break is abrupt, and takes the form of walls and terraces of rock of the most brilliant colour, weathered and stained by ores, and, even under the grey sky, dazzling to the eyes. The driver thought he had understood the directions given, but he was stupid, and once we lost some miles by arriving at a river too rough and deep to be forded, and again we were brought up by an impassable canyon. He grew frightened about his horses, and said no money would ever tempt him into the mountains again; but average intelligence would have made it all easy.

The solitude was becoming sombre, when, after driving for nine hours, and travelling at the least forty-five miles, without any sign of fatigue on the part of the *broncos*, we came to a stream, by the side of which we drove along a definite track, till we came to a sort of tripartite valley, with a majestic crooked canyon 2000 feet deep opening upon it. A rushing stream roared through it, and the Rocky Mountains, with pines scattered over them, came down upon it. A little farther, and the canyon became utterly inaccessible. This was exciting; here was an inner world. A rough and shaky bridge, made of the outsides of pines laid upon some unsecured logs, crossed the river. The *broncos* stopped and smelt it, not liking it, but some encouraging speech induced them to go over. On the other side was a log cabin, partially ruinous, and the very rudest I ever saw, its roof of plastered mud being broken into large holes. It stood close to the water among some cotton-wood trees. A little higher there was a very primitive saw-mill, also out of repair, with some logs lying about. An emigrant waggon and a forlorn tent, with a camp-fire and a pot, were in the foreground, but there was no trace of the boarding-house, of which I stood a little in dread. The driver went for further directions to the log-cabin, and returned with a grim smile deepening the melancholy of his face to say it was Mr Chalmers's, but there was no accommodation for such as him, much less for me! This was truly 'a sell.' I got down and found a single room of the rudest kind, with the wall at one end partially broken down, holes in the roof, holes for windows, and no furniture but two chairs and two unplaned wooden shelves, with some sacks of straw upon them for beds. There was an adjacent cabin room, with a stove, benches, and table, where they cooked and ate, but this was all. A hard, sad-looking woman looked at me measuringly. She said that they sold milk and butter to parties who camped in the canyon, that they had never had any boarders but two asthmatic old ladies, but they would take me for five dollars per week if I 'would make myself agreeable.' The horses had to be fed, and I sat down on a box, had some dried beef and milk, and considered the matter. If I went back to Fort Collins, I thought, I was farther from a mountain life, and had no choice but Denver, a place from which I shrank, or to take the cars for New York. Here the life was rough, rougher than any I had ever seen, and the people repelled me by their faces and manners; but if I could rough it for a few days, I might, I thought, get over canyons and all other difficulties into Estes

Park, which has become the goal of my journey and hopes. So I decided to remain.

September 16

Five days here, and I am no nearer Estes Park. How the days pass I know not; I am weary of the limitations of this existence. This is 'a life in which nothing ever happens.' When the buggy disappeared, I felt as if I had cut the bridge behind me. I sat down and knitted for some time – my usual resource under discouraging circumstances. I really did not know how I should get on. There was no table, no bed, no basin, no towel, no glass, no window, no fastening on the door. The roof was in holes, the logs were unchinked, and one end of the cabin was partially removed! Life was reduced to its simplest elements. I went out; the family all had something to do, and took no notice of me. I went back, and then an awkward girl of sixteen, with uncombed hair, and a painful repulsiveness of face and air, sat on a log for half an hour and stared at me. I tried to draw her into talk, but she twirled her fingers and replied snappishly in monosyllables. Could I by any effort 'make myself agreeable?' I wondered. The day went on. I put on my Hawaiian dress, rolling up the sleeves to the elbows in an 'agreeable' fashion. Towards evening the family returned to feed, and pushed some dried beef and milk in at the door. They all slept under the trees, and before dark carried the sacks of straw out for their bedding. I followed their example that night, or rather watched Charles's Wain while they slept, but since then have slept on blankets on the floor under the roof. They have neither lamp nor candle, so if I want to do anything after dark I have to do it by the unsteady light of pine knots. As the nights are cold, and free from bugs, and I do a good deal of manual labour, I sleep well. At dusk I make my bed on the floor, and draw a bucket of ice-cold water from the river; the family go to sleep under the trees, and I pile logs on the fire sufficient to burn half the night, for I assure you the solitude is *eerie* enough. There are unaccountable noises (wolves), rummagings under the floor, queer cries, and stealthy sounds of I know not what. One night a beast (fox or skunk) rushed in at the open end of [the] cabin, and fled through the window, almost brushing my face, and on another, the head and three or four inches of the body of a snake were protruded through a chink of the floor close to me, to my extreme disgust. My mirror is the polished inside of my watchcase. At sunrise Mrs Chalmers comes in – if coming into a nearly open shed can be called *in* – and makes a fire, because she thinks me too stupid to do it, and mine is the family room; and by seven I am dressed, have folded the blankets, and swept the floor, and then she puts some milk and bread or stirabout on a box by the door. After breakfast I draw more water, and wash one or two garments daily, taking care that there are no witnesses of my inexperience. Yesterday a calf sucked one into hopeless rags. The rest of the day I spend in mending, knitting, writing to you, and the various odds and ends which arise when one has to do all for oneself. At twelve and six some food is put on the box by the door, and at dusk we make up our beds. A distressed emigrant woman has just given birth to a child in a temporary shanty by the river, and I go to help her each day. I have made the acquaintance of all the careworn, struggling settlers within a walk. All have come for health, and most have found or are finding it, even if they have no better shelter than a waggon tilt or a blanket on sticks laid across four poles. The climate of Colorado is considered the finest in North America, and consumptives, asthmatics, dyspeptics, and sufferers from nervous diseases, are here in hundreds and thousands, either trying the 'camp cure' for three or four months, or settling here permanently. People can safely sleep out of doors for six months of the year. The plains are from 4000 to 6000 feet high, and some of the settled 'parks,' or mountain valleys, are from 8000 to 10,000. The air, besides being much rarefied, is very dry. The rainfall is far below the average, dews are rare, and fogs nearly unknown. The sunshine is bright and almost constant, and three-fourths of the days are cloudless. The milk, beef, and bread are good. The climate is neither so hot in summer nor so cold in winter as that of the States, and when the days are hot the nights are cool. Snow rarely lies on the lower ranges, and horses and cattle don't require to be either fed or housed during the winter. Of course the rarefied air quickens respiration. All this is from hearsay. I am not under favourable circumstances, either for mind or body, and at present I feel a singular lassitude and difficulty in taking exercise, but this is said to be the milder form of the affection known on higher altitudes as *soroche*, or 'mountain sickness,' and is only temporary. I am forming a plan for getting farther into the mountains, and hope that my next letter will be more lively. I killed a rattlesnake this morning close to the cabin, and have taken its rattle, which has eleven joints. My life is embittered by the abundance of these reptiles – rattlesnakes and moccasin snakes, both deadly, carpet snakes and 'green racers,' reputed dangerous, water snakes, tree snakes, and mouse snakes, harmless but abominable. Seven rattlesnakes have been killed just outside the cabin since I came. A snake, three feet long, was found coiled under the pillow of the sick woman. I see snakes in all withered twigs, and am ready to flee at 'the sound of a shaken leaf.' And besides snakes, the earth and air are alive and noisy with forms of insect life, large and small, stinging, humming, buzzing, striking, rasping, devouring!

Letter V

Nameless Region, Rocky Mountains, September

This is indeed far removed. It seems farther away from you than any place I have been to yet, except the frozen top of the volcano of Mauna Loa. It is so little profaned by man that if one were compelled to live here in solitude one might truly say of the bears, deer, and elk which abound, 'Their tameness is shocking to me.' It is the world of 'big game.' Just now a heavy-headed elk, with much-branched horns fully three feet long, stood and looked at me, and then quietly trotted away. He was so near that I heard the grass, crisp with hoar frost, crackle under his feet. Bears stripped the cherry-bushes within a few yards of us last night. Now two lovely blue birds, with crests on their heads, are picking about within a stone's-throw. This is 'The Great Lone Land,' until lately the hunting-ground of the Indians, and not yet settled or traversed, or likely to be so, owing to the want of water. A solitary hunter has built a log cabin up here, which he occupies for a few weeks for the purpose of elk-hunting, but all the region is unsurveyed, and mostly unexplored. It is 7 A.M. The sun has not yet risen high enough to melt the hoar-frost, and the air is clear, bright, and cold.

The stillness is profound. I hear nothing but the far-off mysterious roaring of a river in a deep canyon, which we spent two hours last night in trying to find. The horses are lost, and if I were disposed to retort upon my companions the term they invariably apply to me, I should now write, with bitter emphasis, '*that* man' and '*that* woman' have gone in search of them.

The scenery up here is glorious, combining sublimity with beauty, and in the elastic air fatigue has dropped off from me. This is no region for tourists and women, only for a few elk and bear hunters at times, and its unprofaned freshness gives me new life. I cannot by any words give you an idea of scenery so different from any that you or I have ever seen. This is an upland valley of grass and flowers, of glades and sloping lawns, and cherry-fringed beds of dry streams, and clumps of pines artistically placed, and mountain sides densely pine-clad, the pines breaking into fringes as they come down upon the 'park,' and the mountains breaking into pinnacles of bold grey rock as they pierce the blue of the sky. A single dell of bright green grass, on which dwarf clumps of the scarlet poison-oak look like beds of geraniums, slopes towards the west, as if it must lead to the river which we seek. Deep, vast, canyons, all trending westwards, lie in purple gloom. Pine-clad ranges, rising into the blasted top of Storm Peak, all run westwards too, and all the beauty and glory are but the frame out of which rises – heaven-piercing, pure in its pearly lustre, as glorious a mountain as the sun tinges red in either hemisphere – the splintered, pinnacled, lonely, ghastly, imposing, double-peaked summit of Long's Peak, the Mont Blanc of Northern Colorado.

This is a view to which nothing needs to be added. This is truly the 'lodge in some vast wilderness' for which one often sighs when in the midst of 'a bustle at once sordid and trival.' In spite of Dr Johnson, these 'monstrous protuberances' do 'inflame the imagination and elevate the understanding.' This scenery satisfies my soul. Now, the Rocky Mountains realise – nay, exceed – the dream of my childhood. It is magnificent, and the air is life-giving. I should like to spend some time in these higher regions, but I know that this will turn out an abortive expedition, owing to the stupidity and pigheadedness of Chalmers.

There is a most romantic place called Estes Park, at a height of 7500 feet, which can be reached by going down to the plains and then striking up the St Vrain Canyon, but this is a distance of 55 miles, and as Chalmers was confident that he could take me over the mountains, a distance, as he supposed, of about 20 miles, we left at mid-day yesterday, with the fervent hope, on my part, that I might not return. Mrs C. was busy the whole of Tuesday in preparing what she called 'grub,' which, together with 'plenty of bedding,' was to be carried on a pack mule; but when we started I was disgusted to find that Chalmers was on what should have been the pack animal, and that two thickly-quilted cotton 'spreads' had been disposed of under my saddle, making it broad, high, and uncomfortable. Any human being must have laughed to see an expedition start so grotesquely 'ill found.' I had a very old iron-grey horse, whose lower lip hung down feebly, showing his few teeth, while his fore-legs stuck out forwards, and matter ran from both his nearly-blind eyes. It is a kindness to bring him up to abundant pasture. My saddle is an old McLellan cavalry saddle, with a battered brass peak, and the bridle is a rotten leather strap on one side and a strand of rope on the other. The cotton quilts covered the Rosinante from mane to tail. Mrs C. wore an old print skirt, an old short-gown, a print apron, and a sun-bonnet, with the flap coming down to her waist, and looked as careworn and clean as she always does. The inside horn of her saddle was broken; to the outside one hung a saucepan and a bundle of clothes. The one girth was nearly at the breaking-point when we started.

My pack, with my well-worn umbrella upon it, was behind my saddle. I wore my Hawaiian riding-dress, with a handkerchief tied over my face and the sun-cover of my umbrella folded and tied over my hat, for the sun was very fierce. The queerest figure of all was the would-be guide. With his one eye, his gaunt, lean form, and his torn clothes, he looked more like a strolling tinker than the honest worthy settler that he is. He bestrode rather than rode a gaunt mule, whose tail hair had all been shaven off, except a tuft for a tassel at the end. Two flour bags which leaked were tied on behind the saddle, two quilts were under it, and my canvas bag, a battered canteen, a frying-pan, and two lariats hung from the horn. On one foot C. wore an old high boot, into which his trouser was tucked, and on the other an old brogue, through which his toes protruded.

We had an ascent of four hours through a ravine which gradually opened out upon this beautiful 'park,' but we rode through it for some miles before the view burst upon us. The vastness of this range, like astronomical distances, can hardly be conceived of. At this place, I suppose, it is not less than 250 miles wide, and with hardly a break in its continuity, it stretches almost from the Arctic Circle to the Straits of Magellan. From the top of Long's Peak, within a short distance, twenty-two summits, each above 12,000 feet in height, are visible, and the Snowy Range, the backbone or 'divide' of the continent, is seen snaking distinctly through the wilderness of ranges, with its waters starting for either ocean. From the first ridge we crossed after leaving Canyon we had a singular view of range beyond range cleft by deep canyons, and abounding in elliptical valleys, richly grassed. The slopes of all the hills, as far as one could see, were waving with fine grass ready for the scythe, but the food of wild animals only. All these ridges are heavily timbered with pitch pines, and where they come down on the grassy slopes they look as if the trees had been arranged by a landscape gardener. Far off, through an opening in a canyon, we saw the prairie simulating the ocean. Far off, through an opening in another direction, was the glistening outline of the Snowy Range. But still, till we reached this place, it was monotonous, though grand as a whole: a grey-green or buff-grey, with outbreaks of brilliantly-coloured rock, only varied by the black green of pines, which are not the stately pyramidal pines of the Sierra Nevada, but much resemble the natural Scotch fir. Not many miles from us is North Park, a great tract of land said to be rich in gold, but those who have gone to 'prospect' have seldom returned, the region being the home of tribes of Indians who live in perpetual hostility to the whites and to each other.

At this great height, and most artistically situated, we came upon a rude log camp tenanted in winter by an elk hunter, but now deserted. Chalmers without any scruple picked the padlock; we lighted a fire, made some tea, and fried some bacon, and after a good meal mounted again and started for Estes Park. For four weary hours we searched hither and thither along every indentation of the ground which might be supposed to slope towards the Big Thompson River, which we knew had to be forded. Still, as the quest grew more tedious, Long's Peak stood before us as a landmark in purple glory; and still at his feet lay a hollow filled with deep blue atmosphere, where I knew that Estes Park must lie, and still between us and it lay never-lessening miles of inaccessibility, and the sun was ever westering, and the shadows ever lengthening, and Chalmers, who had started confident, bumptious, blatant, was ever becoming more bewildered, and his wife's thin voice more piping and discontented, and my stumbling horse more insecure, and I more determined (as I am at this moment) that somehow or other I would reach that blue hollow, and even stand on Long's Peak where the snow was glittering. Affairs were becoming serious, and Chalmers's incompetence a source of real peril, when, after an exploring expedition, he returned more bumptious than ever, saying he knew it would be all right, he had found a trail, and we could get across the river by dark, and camp out for the night. So he led us into a steep, deep, rough ravine, where we had to dismount, for trees were lying across it everywhere, and there was almost no footing on the great slabs of shelving rock. Yet there was a trail, tolerably well worn, and the branches and twigs near the ground were well broken back. Ah! it was a wild place. My horse fell first, rolling over twice, and breaking off a part of the saddle, in his second roll knocking me over a shelf of three feet of descent. Then Mrs C.'s horse and the mule fell on the top of each other, and on recovering themselves bit each other savagely. The ravine became a wild gulch, the dry bed of some awful torrent; there were huge shelves of rock, great overhanging walls of rock, great prostrate trees, cedar spikes and cacti to wound the feet, and then a precipice fully 500 feet deep! The trail was a trail made by bears in search of bear cherries, which abounded!

It was getting dusk as we had to struggle up the rough gulch we had so fatuously descended. The horses fell several times; I could hardly get mine up at all, though I helped him as much as I could; I was cut and bruised, scratched and torn. A spine of a cactus penetrated my foot, and some vicious thing cut the back of my neck. Poor Mrs C. was much bruised, and I pitied her, for she got no fun out of it as I did. It was an awful climb. When we got out of the gulch, C. was so confused that he took the wrong direction, and after an hour of vague wandering was only recalled to the right one by my pertinacious assertions acting on his weak brain. I was inclined to be angry with the incompetent braggart, who had boasted that he could take us to Estes Park 'blindfold;' but I was sorry for him too, so said nothing, even though I had to walk during these meanderings to save my tired horse. When at last, at dark, we reached the open, there was a snow-flurry, with violent gusts of wind, and the shelter of the camp, dark and cold as it was, was desirable. We had no food, but made a fire. I lay down on some dry grass, with my inverted saddle for a pillow, and slept soundly, till I was awoke by the cold of an intense frost, and the pain of my many cuts and bruises. Chalmers promised that we should make a fresh start at six, so I woke him at five, and here I am alone at half-past eight! I said to him many times that unless he hobbled or picketed the horses, we should lose them. 'Oh,' he said, 'they'll be all right.' In truth he had no picketing-pins. Now, the animals are merrily trotting homewards. I saw them two miles off an hour ago with him after them. His wife, who is also after them, goaded to desperation, said, 'He's the most ignorant, careless, good-for-nothing man I ever saw,' upon which I dwelt upon his being well-meaning. There is a sort of well here, but our 'afternoon tea' and watering the horses drained it, so we have had nothing to drink since yesterday, for the canteen, which started without a cork, lost all its contents when the mule fell. I have made a monstrous fire, but thirst and impatience are hard to bear, and preventible misfortunes are always irksome. I have found the stomach of a bear with fully a pint of cherrystones in it, and have spent an hour in getting the kernels; and lo! now, at half-past nine, I see the culprit and his wife coming back with the animals!

Letter VI

Estes Park!!! September 28

I wish I could let those three notes of admiration go to you instead of a letter. They mean everything that is rapturous and delightful – grandeur, cheerfulness, health, enjoyment, novelty, freedom, etc. etc. I have just dropped into the very place I have been seeking, but in everything it exceeds all my dreams. There is health in every breath of air; I am much better already, and get up to a seven o'clock breakfast without difficulty. It is quite comfortable – in the fashion that I like. I have a log cabin, raised on six posts, all to myself, with a skunk's lair underneath it, and a small lake close to it. There is a frost every night, and all day it is cool enough for a roaring fire. The ranchman, who is half hunter half stockman, and his wife are jovial, hearty Welsh people from Llanberis, who laugh with loud, cheery British laughs, sing in parts down to the youngest child, are free-hearted and hospitable, and pile the pitch-pine logs half-way up the great rude chimney. There has been fresh meat each day since I came, delicious bread baked daily, excellent potatoes, tea and coffee, and an abundant supply of milk like cream. I have a clean hay bed with six blankets, and there are neither bugs nor fleas. The scenery is the most glorious

I have ever seen, and is above us, around us, at the very door. Most people have advised me to go to Colorado Springs, and only one mentioned this place, and till I reached Longmount I never saw any one who had been here, but I saw from the lie of the country that it must be most superbly situated. People said, however, that it was most difficult of access, and that the season for it was over. In travelling there is nothing like dissecting people's statements, which are usually coloured by their estimate of the powers or likings of the person spoken to, making all reasonable inquiries, and then pertinaciously but quietly carrying out one's own plans. This is perfection, and all the requisites for health are present, including plenty of horses and grass to ride on.

It is not easy to sit down to write after ten hours of hard riding, especially in a cabin full of people, and wholesome fatigue may make my letter flat when it ought to be enthusiastic. I was awake all night at Longmount owing to the stifling heat, and got up nervous and miserable, ready to give up the thought of coming here, but the sunrise over the plains, and the wonderful red of the Rocky Mountains, as they reflected the eastern sky, put spirit into me. The landlord had got a horse, but could not give any satisfactory assurances of his being quiet, and being much shaken by my fall at Canyon, I earnestly wished that the *Greeley Tribune* had not given me a reputation for horsemanship, which had preceded me here. The young men who were to escort me 'seemed very innocent,' he said, but I have not arrived at his meaning yet. When the horse appeared in the street at 8.30, I saw, to my dismay, a high-bred, beautiful creature, stable-kept, with arched neck, quivering nostrils, and restless ears and eyes. My pack, as on Hawaii, was strapped behind the Mexican saddle, and my canvas bag hung on the horn, but the horse did not look fit to carry 'gear,' and seemed to require two men to hold and coax him. There were many loafers about, and I shrank from going out and mounting in my old Hawaiian riding-dress, though Dr and Mrs H. assured me that I looked quite 'insignificant and unnoticeable.' We got away at nine with repeated injunctions from the landlord in the words, 'Oh, you should be heroic!'

The sky was cloudless, and a deep brilliant blue, and though the sun was hot the air was fresh and bracing. The ride for glory and delight I shall label along with one to Hanalei, and another to Mauna Kea, Hawaii. I felt better quite soon; the horse in gait and temper turned out perfection – all spring and spirit, elastic in his motion, walking fast and easily, and cantering with a light, graceful swing as soon as one pressed the reins on his neck, a blithe, joyous animal, to whom a day among the mountains seemed a pleasant frolic. So gentle he was, that when I got off and walked he followed me without being led, and without needing any one to hold him he allowed me to mount on either side. In addition to the charm of his movements he has the cat-like sure-footedness of a Hawaiian horse, and fords rapid and rough-bottomed rivers, and gallops among stones and stumps, and down steep hills, with equal security. I could have ridden him a hundred miles as easily as twenty-five and a half. We have only been together two days, yet we are firm friends, and thoroughly understand each other. I should not require another companion on a long mountain tour. All his ways are those of an animal brought up without curb, whip, or spur, trained by the voice, and used only to kindness, as is happily the case with the majority of horses in the Western States. Consequently, unless they are *broncos*, they exercise their intelligence for your advantage, and do their work rather as friends than as machines.

I soon began not only to feel better, but to be exhilarated with the delightful motion. The sun was behind us, and puffs of a cool elastic air came down from the glorious mountains in front. We cantered across six miles of prairie, and then reached the beautiful canyon of the St Vrain, which, towards its mouth, is a narrow, fertile, wooded valley, through which a bright rapid river, which we forded many times, hurries along, with twists and windings innumerable. Ah, how brightly its ripples danced in the glittering sunshine, and how musically its waters murmured like the streams of windward Hawaii! We lost our way over and over again, though the 'innocent' young men had been there before; indeed, it would require some talent to master the intricacies of that devious trail, but settlers making hay always appeared in the nick of time to put us on the right track. Very fair it was, after the brown and burning plains, and the variety was endless. Cottonwood trees were green and bright, aspens shivered in golden tremulousness, wild grape-vines trailed their lemon-coloured foliage along the ground, and the

Virginia creeper hung its crimson sprays here and there, lighting up green and gold into glory. Sometimes from under the cool and bowery shade of the coloured tangle we passed into the cool St Vrain, and then were wedged between its margin and lofty cliffs and terraces of incredibly staring, fantastic rocks, lined, patched, and splashed with carmine, vermilion, greens of all tints, blue, yellow, orange, violet, deep crimson, colouring that no artist would dare to represent, and of which, in sober prose, I scarcely dare tell. Long's wonderful peaks, which hitherto had gleamed above the green, now disappeared, to be seen no more for twenty miles. We entered on an ascending valley, where the gorgeous hues of the rocks were intensified by the blue gloom of the pitch-pines, and then taking a track to the north-west, we left the softer world behind, and all traces of man and his works, and plunged into the Rocky Mountains.

There were wonderful ascents then up which I led my horse: wild fantastic views opening up continually, a recurrence of surprises; the air keener and purer with every mile, the sensation of loneliness more singular. A tremendous ascent among rocks and pines to a height of 9000 feet brought us to a passage seven feet wide through a wall of rock, with an abrupt descent of 2000 feet, and a yet higher ascent beyond. I never saw anything so strange as looking back. It was a single gigantic ridge which we had passed through, standing up knife-like, built up entirely of great brick-shaped masses of bright red rock, some of them as large as the Royal Institution, Edinburgh, piled one on another by

Titans. Pitch-pines grew out of their crevices, but there was not a vestige of soil. Beyond, wall beyond wall of similar construction, and range above range, rose into the blue sky. Fifteen miles more over great ridges, along passes dark with shadow, and so narrow that we had to ride in the beds of the streams which had excavated them, round the bases of colossal pyramids of rock crested with pines, up into fair upland 'parks,' scarlet in patches with the poison oak, parks so beautifully arranged by nature that I momentarily expected to come upon some stately mansion, but that afternoon crested blue jays and chipmonks had them all to themselves. Here, in the early morning, deer, bighorn, and the stately elk, come down to feed, and there, in the night, prowl and growl the Rocky Mountain lion, the grizzly bear, and the cowardly wolf. There were chasms of immense depth, dark with the indigo gloom of pines, and mountains with snow gleaming on their splintered crests, loveliness to bewilder and grandeur to awe, and still streams and shady pools, and cool depths of shadow; mountains again, dense with pines, among which patches of aspen gleamed like gold; valleys where the yellow cottonwood mingled with the crimson oak, and so, on and on through the lengthening shadows, till the trail, which in places had been hardly legible, became well defined, and we entered a long gulch with broad swellings of grass belted with pines.

A very pretty mare, hobbled, was feeding; a collie dog barked at us, and among the scrub, not far from the track, there was a rude, black log cabin, as rough as it could be to be a shelter at all, with smoke coming out of the roof and window. We diverged towards it; it mattered not that it was the home, or rather den, of a notorious 'ruffian' and 'desperado.' One of my companions had disappeared hours before, the remaining one was a town-bred youth. I longed to speak to some one who loved the mountains. I called the hut a *den* – it looked like the den of a wild beast. The big dog lay outside it in a threatening attitude and growled. The mud roof was covered with lynx, beaver, and other furs laid out to dry, beaver paws were pinned out on the logs, a part of the carcass of a deer hung at one end of the cabin, a skinned beaver lay in front of a heap of peltry just within the door, and antlers of deer, old horseshoes, and offal of many animals, lay about the den. Roused by the growling of the dog, his owner came out, a broad, thickset man, about the middle height, with an old cap on his head, and wearing a grey hunting-suit much the worse for wear (almost falling to pieces, in fact), a digger's scarf knotted round his waist, a knife in his belt, and 'a bosom friend,' a revolver, sticking out of the breast-pocket of his coat; his feet, which were very small, were bare, except for some dilapidated moccasins made of horse hide. The marvel was how his clothes hung together, and on him. The scarf round his waist must have had something to do with it. His face was remarkable. He is a man about forty-five, and must have been strikingly handsome. He has large grey-blue eyes, deeply set, with well-marked eyebrows, a handsome aquiline nose, and a very handsome mouth. His face was smooth-shaven except for a dense moustache and imperial. Tawny hair, in thin uncared-for curls, fell from under his hunter's cap and over his collar. One eye was entirely gone, and the loss made one side of the face repulsive, while the other might have been modelled in marble. 'Desperado' was written in large letters all over him. I almost repented of having sought his acquaintance. His first impulse was to swear at the dog, but on seeing a lady he contented himself with kicking him, and coming up to me he raised his cap, showing as he did so a magnificently-formed brow and head, and in a cultured tone of voice asked if there were anything he could do for me? I asked for some water, and he brought some in a battered tin, gracefully apologising for not having anything more presentable. We entered into conversation, and as he spoke I forgot both his reputation and appearance, for his manner was that of a chivalrous gentleman, his accent refined, and his language easy and elegant. I inquired about some beavers' paws which were drying, and in a moment they hung on the horn of my saddle. *Apropos* of the wild animals of the region, he told me that the loss of his eye was owing to a recent encounter with a grizzly bear, which, after giving him a death hug, tearing him all over, breaking his arm and scratching out his eye, had left him for dead. As we rode away, for the sun was sinking, he said, courteously, 'You are not an American. I know from your voice that you are a countrywoman of mine. I hope you will allow me the pleasure of calling on you.' This man, known through the Territories and beyond them as 'Rocky Mountain Jim,' or, more briefly, as 'Mountain Jim,' is one of the famous scouts of the Plains, and is the original of some daring portraits in fiction concerning Indian frontier warfare. So far as I have at present heard, he is a man for whom there is now no room, for the time for blows and blood in this part of Colorado is past, and the fame of many daring exploits is sullied by crimes which are not easily forgiven here. He now has a 'squatter's claim,' but makes his living as a trapper, and is a complete child of the mountains. Of his genius and chivalry to women there does not appear to be any doubt; but he is a desperate character, and is subject to 'ugly fits,' when people think it best to avoid him. It is here regarded as an evil that he has located himself at the mouth of the only entrance to the Park, for he is dangerous with his pistols, and it would be safer if he were not here. His besetting sin is indicated in the verdict pronounced on him by my host: 'When he's sober Jim's a perfect gentleman; but when he's had liquor he's the most awful ruffian in Colorado.'

From the ridge on which this gulch terminates, at a height of 9000 feet, we saw at last Estes Park, lying 1500 feet below in the glory of the setting sun, an irregular basin, lighted up by the bright waters of the rushing Thompson, guarded by sentinel mountains of fantastic shape and monstrous size, with Long's Peak rising above them all in unapproachable grandeur, while the Snowy Range, with its outlying spurs heavily timbered, come down upon the Park slashed by stupendous canyons lying deep in purple gloom. The rushing river was blood-red, Long's Peak was aflame, the glory of the glowing heaven was given back from earth. Never, nowhere, have I seen anything to equal the view into Estes Park. The mountains 'of the land which is very far off' are very near now, but the near is more glorious than the far, and reality than dreamland. The mountain fever seized me, and, giving my tireless horse one encouraging word, he dashed at full gallop over a mile of smooth sward at delirious speed. But I was hungry, and the air was frosty, and I was wondering what the prospects of food and shelter were in this enchanted region, when we came suddenly upon a small lake, close to which was a very trim-looking log cabin, with a flat mud roof, with four smaller ones; picturesquely dotted about near it, two *corrals*, a long shed, in front of which a steer was being killed, a log-dairy with a water-wheel, some hay-piles, and various evidences of comfort; and two men, on serviceable horses, were just bringing in some tolerable cows to be milked. A short, pleasant-looking man ran up to me and shook hands gleefully, which surprised me; but he has since told me that in the evening light he thought I was 'Mountain Jim, dressed up as a woman!' I recognised in him a countryman, and he introduced himself as Griffith Evans, a Welshman from the slate quarries near Llanberis. When the cabin-door was opened I saw a good-sized log room, unchinked, however, with windows of infamous glass, looking two ways; a rough stone fireplace, in which pine logs, half as large as I am, were burning; a boarded floor, a round table, two rocking-chairs, a carpet-covered backwoods couch; and skins, Indian bows and arrows, wampum belts, and antlers, fitly decorated the rough walls, and equally fitly rifles were stuck up in the corners. Seven men, smoking, were lying about on the floor, a sick man lay on the couch, and a middle-aged lady sat at the table writing. I went out again and asked Evans if he could take me in, expecting nothing better than a shakedown; but, to my joy, he told me he could give me a cabin to myself, two minutes' walk from his own. So in this glorious upper world, with the mountain pines behind and the clear lake in front, in the 'blue hollow at the foot of Long's Peak,' at a height of 7500 feet, where the hoar frost crisps the grass every night of the year, I have found far more than I ever dared to hope for.

Letter VII

Estes Park, Colorado, October

Long's Peak, 14,700 feet high, blocks up one end of Estes Park, and dwarfs all the surrounding mountains. From it on this side rise, snow-born, the bright St Vrain, and the Big and Little Thompson. By sunlight or moonlight its splintered grey crest is the one object which, in spite of wapiti and bighorn, skunk and grizzly, unfailingly arrests the eye. From it come all storms of snow and wind, and the forked lightnings play round its head like a glory. It is one of the noblest of mountains, but in one's imagination it grows to be much more than a mountain. It becomes invested with a personality. In its caverns and abysses one comes to fancy that it generates and chains the strong winds, to let them loose in its fury. The thunder becomes its voice, and the lightnings do it homage. Other summits blush under the morning kiss of the sun, and turn pale the next moment; but it detains the first sunlight and holds it round its head for an hour at least, till it pleases to change from rosy red to deep blue; and the sunset, as if spell-bound, lingers latest on its crest. The soft winds which hardly rustle the pine needles down here are raging rudely up there round its motionless summit. The mark of fire is upon it; and though it has passed into a grim repose, it tells of fire and upheaval as truly, though not as eloquently, as the living volcanoes of Hawaii. Here under its shadow one learns how naturally nature worship, and the propitiation of the forces of nature arose in minds which had no better light.

Long's Peak, 'the American Matterhorn,' as some call it, was ascended five years ago for the first time. I thought I should like to attempt it, but up to Monday, when Evans left for Denver, cold water was thrown upon the project. It was too late in the season, the winds were likely to be strong, etc.; but just before leaving, Evans said that the weather was looking more settled, and if I did not get farther than the timber line it would be worth going. Soon after he left, 'Mountain Jim' came in, and said he would go up as guide, and the two youths who rode here with me from Longmount and I caught at the proposal. Mrs Edwards at once baked bread for three days, steaks were cut from the steer which hangs up conveniently, and tea, sugar, and butter were benevolently added. Our picnic was not to be a luxurious or 'well-found' one, for, in order to avoid the expense of a pack mule, we limited our luggage to what our saddle horses could carry. Behind my saddle I carried three pair of camping blankets and a quilt, which reached to my shoulders. My own boots were so much worn that it was painful to walk, even about the park, in them, so Evans had lent me a pair of his hunting boots, which hung to the horn of my saddle. The horses of the two young men were equally loaded, for we had to prepare for many degrees of frost. 'Jim' was a shocking figure; he had on an old pair of high boots, with a baggy pair of old trousers made of deer hide, held on by an old scarf tucked into them; a leather shirt, with three or four ragged unbuttoned waistcoats over it; an old smashed wideawake, from under which his tawny, neglected ringlets hung; and with his one eye, his one long spur, his knife in his belt, his revolver in his waistcoat pocket, his saddle covered with an old beaver-skin, from which the paws hung down; his camping blankets behind him, his rifle laid across the saddle in front of him, and his axe, canteen, and other gear hanging to the horn, he was as awful-looking a ruffian as one could see. By way of contrast he rode a small Arab mare, of exquisite beauty, skittish, high-spirited, gentle, but altogether too light for him, and he fretted her incessantly to make her display herself.

Heavily loaded as all our horses were, 'Jim' started over the half-mile of level grass at a hand-gallop, and then throwing his mare on her haunches, pulled up alongside of me, and with a grace of manner which soon made me forget his appearance, entered into a conversation which lasted for more than three hours, in spite of the manifold checks of fording streams, single file, abrupt ascents and descents, and other incidents of mountain travel. The ride was one series of glories and surprises, of 'park' and glade, of lake and stream, of mountains on mountains, culminating in the rent pinnacles of Long's Peak, which looked yet grander and ghastlier as we crossed an attendant mountain 11,000 feet high. The slanting sun added fresh beauty every hour. There were dark pines against a lemon sky, grey peaks reddening and etherealising, gorges of deep and infinite blue, floods of golden glory pouring through canyons of enormous depth, an atmosphere of absolute purity, an occasional foreground of cotton-wood and aspen flaunting in red and gold to intensify the blue gloom of the pines, the trickle and murmur of streams fringed with icicles, the strange *sough* of gusts moving among the pine tops – sights and sounds not of the lower earth, but of the solitary, beast-haunted, frozen upper altitudes. From the dry, buff grass of Estes Park we turned off up a trail on the side of a pine-hung gorge, up a steep pine-clothed hill, down to a small valley, rich in fine, sun-cured hay about eighteen inches high, and enclosed by high mountains whose deepest hollow contains a lily-covered lake, fitly named 'The Lake of the Lilies.' Ah, how magical its beauty was, as it slept in silence, while *there* the dark pines were mirrored motionless in its pale gold, and *here* the great white lily cups and dark green leaves rested on amethyst-coloured water!

From this we ascended into the purple gloom of great pine forests which clothe the skirts of the mountains up to a height of about 11,000 feet, and from their chill and solitary depths we had glimpses of golden atmosphere and rose-lit summits, not of 'the land very far off,' but of the land nearer now in all its grandeur, gaining in sublimity by nearness – glimpses, too, through a broken vista of purple gorges, of the illimitable Plains lying idealised in the late sunlight, their baked, brown expanse transfigured into the likeness of a sunset sea rolling infinitely in waves of misty gold.

We rode upwards through the gloom on a steep trail blazed through the forest, all my intellect concentrated on avoiding being dragged off my horse by impending branches, or having the blankets badly torn, as those of my companions were, by sharp dead limbs, between which there was hardly room to pass – the horses breathless, and requiring to stop every few yards, though their riders, except myself, were afoot. The gloom of the dense, ancient, silent forest is to me awe-inspiring. On such an evening it is soundless, except for the branches creaking in the soft wind, the frequent snap of decayed timber, and a murmur in the pine tops as of a not distant waterfall, all tending to produce *eeriness* and a sadness 'hardly akin to pain.' There no lumberer's axe has ever rung. The trees die when they have attained their prime, and stand there, dead and bare, till the fierce mountain winds lay them prostrate. The pines grew smaller and more sparse as we ascended, and the last stragglers wore a tortured, warring look. The timber line was passed, but yet a little higher a slope of mountain meadow dipped to the south-west towards a bright stream trickling under ice and icicles, and there a grove of the beautiful silver spruce marked our camping ground. The trees were in miniature, but so exquisitely arranged that one might well ask what artist's hand had planted them, scattering them here, clumping them there, and training their slim spires towards heaven. Hereafter, when I call up memories of the glorious, the view from this camping ground will come up. Looking east, gorges opened to the distant Plains, then fading into purple grey.

Mountains with pine-clothed skirts rose in ranges, or, solitary, uplifted their grey summits, while close behind, but nearly 3000 feet above us, towered the bald white crest of Long's Peak, its huge precipices red with the light of a sun long lost to our eyes. Close to us, in the caverned side of the Peak, was snow that, owing to its position, is eternal. Soon the after-glow came on, and before it faded a big half-moon hung out of the heavens, shining through the silver blue foliage of the pines on the frigid background of snow, and turning the whole into fairyland.

[. . .]

Unsaddling and picketing the horses securely, making the beds of pine shoots, and dragging up logs for fuel, warmed us all. 'Jim' built up a great fire, and before long we were all sitting round it at supper. It didn't matter much that we had to drink our tea out of the battered meat-tins in which it was boiled, and eat strips of beef reeking with pine smoke without plates or forks.

'Treat Jim as a gentleman and you'll find him one,' I had been told; and though his manner was certainly bolder and freer than that of gentlemen generally, no imaginary fault could be found. He was very agreeable as a man of culture as well as a child of nature; the desperado was altogether out of sight. He was very courteous and even kind to me, which was fortunate, as the young men had little idea of showing even ordinary civilities. That night I made the acquaintance of his dog 'Ring,' said to be the best hunting-dog in

Colorado, with the body and legs of a collie, but a head approaching that of a mastiff, a noble face with a wistful human expression, and the most truthful eyes I ever saw in an animal. His master loves him if he loves anything, but in his savage moods ill-treats him. 'Ring's' devotion never swerves, and his truthful eyes are rarely taken off his master's face. He is almost human in his intelligence, and, unless he is told to do so, he never takes notice of any one but 'Jim.' In a tone as if speaking to a human being, his master pointing to me, said, 'Ring, go to that lady, and don't leave her again to-night.' 'Ring' at once came to me, looked into my face, laid his head on my shoulder and then lay down beside me with his head on my lap, but never taking his eyes from 'Jim's' face.

The long shadows of the pines lay upon the frosted grass, an aurora leaped fitfully, and the moonlight, though intensely bright, was pale beside the red, leaping flames of our pine logs and their red glow on our gear, ourselves, and 'Ring's' truthful face. One of the young men sang a Latin student's song and two negro melodies; the other, 'Sweet Spirit, hear my Prayer.' 'Jim' sang one of Moore's melodies in a singular falsetto, and all together sang 'The Star-spangled Banner' and 'The Red, White, and Blue.' Then 'Jim' recited a very clever poem of his own composition, and told some fearful Indian stories. A group of small silver spruces away from the fire was my sleeping-place. The artist who had been up there had so woven and interlaced their lower inches as to form a bower, affording at once shelter from the wind and a most agreeable privacy. It was thickly strewn with young pine shoots, and these, when covered with a blanket, with an inverted saddle for a pillow, made a luxurious bed. The mercury at 9 P.M. was 12° below the freezing point. 'Jim,' after a last look at the horses, made a huge fire, and stretched himself out beside it, but 'Ring' lay at my back to keep me warm. I could not sleep, but the night passed rapidly. I was anxious about the ascent, for gusts of ominous sound swept through the pines at intervals. Then wild animals howled, and 'Ring' was perturbed in spirit about them. Then it was strange to see the notorious desperado, a red-handed man, sleeping as quietly as innocence sleeps. But, above all, it was exciting to lie there, with no better shelter than a bower of pines, on a mountain 11,000 feet high, in the very heart of the Rocky Range, under twelve degrees of frost, hearing sounds of wolves, with shivering stars looking through the fragrant canopy, with arrowy pines for bed-posts, and for a night lamp the red flames of a camp fire.

Day dawned long before the sun rose, pure and lemon-coloured. The rest were looking after the horses, when one of the students came running to tell me that I must come farther down the slope, for 'Jim' said he had never seen such a sunrise. From the chill, grey Peak above, from the everlasting snows, from the silvered pines, down through mountain ranges with their depths of Tyrian purple, we looked to where the Plains lay cold, in blue grey, like a morning sea against a far horizon. Suddenly, as a dazzling streak at first, but enlarging rapidly into a dazzling sphere, the sun wheeled above the grey line, a light and glory as when it was first created. 'Jim' involuntarily and reverently uncovered his head, and exclaimed, 'I believe there is a God!' I felt as if, Parsee-like, I must worship. The grey of the Plains changed to purple, the sky was all one rose-red flush, on which vermilion cloud-streaks rested; the ghastly peaks gleamed like rubies, the earth and heavens were new-created. Surely 'the Most High dwelleth not in temples made with hands!' For a full hour those Plains simulated the ocean, down to whose limitless expanse of purple, cliffs, rocks, and promontories swept down.

By seven we had finished breakfast, and passed into the ghastlier solitudes above, I riding as far as what, rightly or wrongly, are called the 'Lava Beds,' an expanse of large and small boulders, with snow in their crevices. It was very cold; some water which we crossed was frozen hard enough to bear the horse. 'Jim' had advised me against taking any wraps, and my thin Hawaiian riding-dress, only fit for the tropics, was penetrated by the keen air. The rarefied atmosphere soon began to oppress our breathing, and I found that Evans's boots were so large that I had no foothold. Fortunately, before the real difficulty of the ascent began, we found, under a rock, a pair of small over-shoes, probably left by the Hayden exploring expedition, which just lasted for the day. As we were leaping from rock to rock, 'Jim' said, 'I was thinking in the night about your travelling alone, and wondering where you carried your Derringer, for I could see no signs of it.' On my telling him that I travelled unarmed, he could hardly believe it, and adjured me to get a revolver at once.

On arriving at the 'Notch' (a literal gate of rock), we found ourselves absolutely on the knife-like ridge or backbone of Long's Peak, only a few feet wide, covered with colossal boulders and fragments, and on the other side shelving in one precipitous, snow-patched sweep of 3000 feet to a picturesque hollow, containing a lake of pure green water. Other lakes, hidden among dense pine woods, were farther off, while close above us rose the Peak, which, for about 500 feet, is a smooth, gaunt, inaccessible-looking pile of granite. Passing through the 'Notch,' we looked along the nearly inaccessible side of the Peak, composed of boulders and *dêbris* of all shapes and sizes, through which appeared broad, smooth ribs of reddish-coloured granite, looking as if they upheld the towering rock-mass above. I usually dislike bird's-eye and panoramic views, but, though from a mountain, this was not one. Serrated ridges, not much lower than that on which we stood, rose, one beyond another, far as that pure atmosphere could carry the vision, broken into awful chasms deep with ice and snow, rising into pinnacles piercing the heavenly blue with their cold, barren grey, on, on for ever, till the most distant range upbore unsullied snow alone. There were fair lakes mirroring the dark pine woods, canyons dark and blue-black with unbroken expanses of pines, snow-slashed pinnacles, wintry heights frowning upon lovely parks, watered and wooded, lying in the lap of summer; North Park floating off into the blue distance, Middle Park closed till another season, the sunny slopes of Estes Park, and winding down among the mountains the snowy ridge of the Divide, whose bright waters seek both the Atlantic and Pacific Oceans. There, far below, links of diamonds showed where the Grand River takes its rise to seek the mysterious Colorado, with its still unsolved enigma, and lose itself in the waters of the Pacific; and nearer the snow-born Thompson bursts forth from the ice to begin its journey to the Gulf of Mexico. Nature, rioting in her grandest mood, exclaimed with voices of grandeur, solitude, sublimity, beauty, and infinity, 'Lord, what is man, that Thou art mindful of him? or the son of man, that Thou visitest him?' Never-to-be-forgotten glories they were, burnt in upon my memory by six succeeding hours of terror. You know I have no head and no ankles, and never ought to dream of mountaineering; and had I known that the ascent was a real mountaineering feat I should not have felt the slightest ambition to perform it. As it is, I am only humiliated by my success, for 'Jim' dragged me up, like a bale of goods, by sheer force of muscle. At the 'Notch' the real business of the ascent began. Two thousand feet of solid rock towered above us, four thousand feet of broken rock shelved precipitously below; smooth granite ribs, with barely a foothold, stood out here and there; melted snow, refrozen several times, presented a more serious obstacle; many of the rocks were loose, and tumbled down when touched. To me it was a time of extreme terror. I was roped to 'Jim,' but it was of no use, my feet were paralysed and slipped on the bare rock, and he said it was useless to try to go that way, and we retraced our steps. I wanted to return to the 'Notch', knowing that my incompetence would detain the party, and one of the young men said almost plainly that a woman was a dangerous encumbrance, but the trapper replied shortly that if it were not to take a lady up he would not go up at all. He went on to explore and reported that further progress on the correct line of ascent was blocked by ice; and then for two hours we descended, lowering ourselves by our hands from rock to rock along a boulder-strewn sweep of 4000 feet, patched with ice and snow, and perilous from rolling stones. My fatigue, giddiness, and pain from bruised ankles, and arms half pulled out of their sockets, were so great that I should never have gone half-way had not 'Jim,' *nolens volens*, dragged me along with a patience and skill, and withal a determination that I should ascend the Peak, which never failed. After descending about 2000 feet to avoid the ice, we got into a deep ravine with inaccessible sides, partly filled with ice and snow and partly with large and small fragments of rock, which were constantly giving way, rendering the footing very insecure. That part to me was two hours of painful and unwilling submission to the inevitable; of trembling, slipping, straining, of smooth ice appearing when it was least expected, and of weak entreaties to be left behind while the others went on. 'Jim' always said that there was no danger, that there was only a short bad bit ahead, and that I should go up even if he carried me!

Slipping, faltering, gasping from the exhausting toil in the rarefied air, with throbbing hearts and panting lungs, we reached the top of the gorge and squeezed ourselves between two gigantic fragments of rock by a passage called the 'Dog's Lift,' when I climbed on the shoulders of one man and then was hauled up. This introduced us by an abrupt turn round the south-west angle of the Peak to a narrow shelf of considerable length, rugged, uneven, and so overhung by the cliff in some places that it is necessary to crouch to pass at all. Above, the Peak looks nearly vertical for 400 feet; and below, the most tremendous precipice I have ever seen descends in one unbroken fall. This is usually considered the most dangerous part of the ascent, but it does not seem so to me, for such foothold as there is is secure, and one fancies that it is possible to hold on with the hands. But there, and on the final, and, to my thinking, the worst part of the climb, one slip, and a breathing, thinking, human being would lie 3000 feet below, a shapeless, bloody heap! 'Ring' refused to traverse the Ledge, and remained at the 'Lift' howling piteously.

From thence the view is more magnificent even than that from the 'Notch.' At the foot of the precipice below us lay a lovely lake, wood embosomed, from or near which the bright St Vrain and other streams take their rise. I thought how their clear cold waters, growing turbid in the affluent flats, would heat under the tropic sun, and eventually form part of that great ocean river which renders our far-off islands habitable by impinging on their shores. Snowy ranges, one behind the other, extended to the distant horizon, folding in their wintry embrace the beauties of Middle Park.

Pike's Peak, more than one hundred miles off, lifted that vast but shapeless summit which is the landmark of Southern Colorado. There were snow patches, snow slashes, snow abysses, snow forlorn and soiled-looking, snow pure and dazzling, snow glistening above the purple robe of pine worn by all the mountains; while away to the east, in limitless breadth, stretched the green-grey of the endless Plains. Giants everywhere reared their splintered crests. From thence, with a single sweep, the eye takes in a distance of 300 miles – that distance to the west, north, and south being made up of mountains ten, eleven, twelve, and thirteen thousand feet in height, dominated by Long's Peak, Gray's Peak, and Pike's Peak, all nearly the height of Mont Blanc! On the Plains we traced the rivers by their fringe of cotton-woods to the distant Platte, and between us and them lay glories of mountain, canyon, and lake, sleeping in depths of blue and purple most ravishing to the eye.

As we crept from the lodge round a horn of rock, I beheld what made me perfectly sick and dizzy to look at – the terminal Peak itself – a smooth, cracked face or wall of pink granite, as nearly perpendicular as anything could well be up which it was possible to climb, well deserving the name of the 'American Matterhorn.'

Scaling, not climbing, is the correct term for this last ascent. It took one hour to accomplish 500 feet, pausing for breath every minute or two. The only foothold was in narrow cracks or on minute projections on the granite. To get a toe in these cracks, or here and there on a scarcely obvious projection, while crawling on hands and knees, all the while tortured with thirst and gasping and struggling for breath, this was the climb; but at last the Peak was won. A grand, well-defined mountain-top it is, a nearly level acre of boulders, with precipitous sides all round, the one we came up being the only accessible one.

It was not possible to remain long. One of the young men was seriously alarmed by bleeding from the lungs, and the intense dryness of the day and the rarefaction of the air, at a height of nearly 15,000 feet, made respiration very painful. There is always water on the Peak, but it was frozen as hard as a rock, and the sucking of ice and snow increases thirst. We all suffered severely from the want of water, and the gasping for breath made our mouths and tongues so dry that articulation was difficult, and the speech of all unnatural.

From the summit were seen in unrivalled combination all the views which had rejoiced our eyes during the ascent. It was something at last to stand upon the storm-rent crown of this lonely sentinel of the Rocky Range, on one of the mightiest of the vertebræ of the backbone of the North American continent, and to see the waters start for both oceans. Uplifted above love and hate and storms of passion, calm amidst the eternal silences, fanned by zephyrs and bathed in living blue, peace rested for that one bright day on the Peak, as if it were some region

> Where falls not rain, or hail, or any snow,
> Or ever wind blows loudly.

We placed our names, with the date of ascent, in a tin within a crevice, and descended to the Ledge, sitting on the smooth granite, getting our feet into cracks and against projections, and letting ourselves down by our hands, 'Jim' going before me, so that I might steady my feet against his powerful shoulders. I was no longer giddy, and faced the precipice of 3500 feet without a shiver. Repassing the Ledge and Lift, we accomplished the descent through 1500 feet of ice and snow, with many falls and bruises, but no worse mishap, and there separated, the young men taking the steepest but most direct way to the Notch, with the intention of getting ready for the march home, and 'Jim' and I taking what he thought the safer route for me – a descent over boulders for 2000 feet, and then a tremendous ascent to the 'Notch.' I had various falls, and once hung by my frock, which caught on a rock, and 'Jim' severed it with his hunting-knife, upon which I fell into a crevice full of soft snow. We were driven lower down the mountains than he had intended by impassable tracts of ice, and the ascent was tremendous. For the last 200 feet the boulders were of enormous size, and the steepness fearful. Sometimes I drew myself up on hands and knees, sometimes crawled; sometimes 'Jim' pulled me up by my arms or a lariat, and sometimes I stood on his shoulders, or he made steps for me of his feet and hands, but at six we stood on the Notch in the splendour of the sinking sun, all colour deepening, all peaks glorifying, all shadows purpling, all peril past.

'Jim' had parted with his *brusquerie* when we parted from the students, and was gentle and considerate beyond anything, though I knew that he must be grievously disappointed, both in my courage and strength. Water was an object of earnest desire. My tongue rattled in my mouth, and I could hardly articulate. It is good for one's sympathies to have for once a severe experience of thirst. Truly, there was

> Water, water, everywhere,
> But not a drop to drink.

Three times its apparent gleam deceived even the mountaineer's practised eye, but we found only a foot of 'glare ice.' At last, in a deep hole, he succeeded in breaking the ice, and by putting one's arm far down one could scoop up a little water in one's hand, but it was tormentingly insufficient. With great difficulty and much assistance I recrossed the 'Lava Beds,' was carried to the horse and lifted upon him, and when we reached the camping ground I was lifted off him, and laid on the ground wrapped up in blankets, a humiliating termination of a great exploit. The horses were saddled, and the young men were all ready to start, but 'Jim' quietly said, 'Now, gentlemen, I want a good night's rest, and we shan't stir from here to-night.' I believe they were really glad to have it so, as one of them was quite 'finished.' I retired to my arbour, wrapped myself in a roll of blankets, and was soon asleep. When I woke, the moon was high shining through the silvery branches, whitening the bald Peak above, and glittering on the great abyss of snow behind, and pine logs were blazing like a bonfire in the cold still air. My feet were so icy cold that I could not sleep again, and getting some blankets to sit in, and making a roll of them for my back, I sat for two hours by the camp fire. It was weird and gloriously beautiful. The students were asleep not far off in their blankets with their feet towards the fire. 'Ring' lay on one side of me with his fine head on my arm, and his master sat smoking, with the fire lighting up the handsome side of his face, and except for the tones of our voices, and an occasional crackle and splutter as a pine knot blazed up, there was no sound on the mountain side. The beloved stars of my far-off home were overhead, the Plough and Pole Star, with their steady light; the glittering Pleiades, looking larger than I ever saw them, and 'Orion's studded belt' shining gloriously. Once only some wild animals prowled near the camp, when 'Ring,' with one bound, disappeared from my side; and the horses, which were picketed by the stream, broke their lariats, stampeded, and came rushing wildly towards the fire, and it was fully half an hour before they were caught and quiet was restored. 'Jim,' or Mr Nugent, as I always scrupulously called him, told stories of his early youth, and of a great sorrow which had led him to embark on a lawless and desperate life. His voice trembled, and tears rolled down his cheek. Was it semi-conscious acting, I wondered, or was his dark soul really stirred to its depths by the silence, the beauty, and the memories of youth?

We reached Estes Park at noon of the following day. A more successful ascent of the Peak was never made, and I would not now exchange my memories of its perfect beauty and extraordinary sublimity for any other experience of mountaineering in any part of the world. Yesterday snow fell on the summit, and it will be inaccessible for eight months to come.

Letter VIII

Estes Park, Colorado Territory, October 2

How time has slipped by I do not know. This is a glorious region, and the air and life are intoxicating. I live mainly out of doors and on horseback, wear my half threadbare Hawaiian dress, sleep sometimes under the stars on a bed of pine boughs, ride on a Mexican saddle, and hear once more the low music of my Mexican spurs. 'There's a stranger! Heave arf a brick at him!' is said by many travellers to express the feeling of the new settlers in these Territories. This is not my experience in my cheery mountain home. How the rafters ring as I write with songs and mirth, while the pitch-pine logs blaze and crackle in the chimney, and the fine snow-dust drives in through the chinks and forms mimic snow-wreaths on the floor, and the wind raves and howls and plays among the creaking pine branches and snaps them short off, and the lightning plays round the blasted top of Long's Peak, and the hardy hunters divert themselves with the thought that when I go to bed I must turn out and face the storm!

[. . .]

The ranchmen are two Welshmen, Evans and Edwards, each with a wife and family. The men are as diverse as they can be. 'Griff,' as Evans is called, is short and small, and is hospitable, careless, reckless, jolly, social, convivial, peppery, good-natured, 'nobody's enemy but his own.' He had the wit and taste to find out Estes Park, where people have found him out, and have induced him to give them food and lodging, and add cabin to cabin to take them in. He is a splendid shot, an expert and successful hunter, a bold mountaineer, a good rider, a capital cook, and a generally 'jolly fellow.' His cheery laugh rings through the cabin from the early morning, and is contagious, and when the rafters ring at night with such songs as 'D'ye ken John Peel?,' 'Auld Lang Syne,' and 'John Brown,' what would the chorus be without poor 'Griff's' voice? What would Estes Park be without him, indeed? When he went to Denver lately, we missed him as we should have missed the sunshine, and perhaps more. In the early morning, when Long's Peak is red, and the grass crackles with the hoar-frost, he arouses me with a cheery thump on my door. 'We're going cattle-hunting, will you come?' or, 'Will you help to drive in the cattle? you can take your pick of the horses. I want another hand.' Free-hearted, lavish, popular, poor 'Griff' loves liquor too well for his prosperity, and is always tormented by debt. He makes lots of money, but puts it into 'a bag with holes.' He has fifty horses and 1000 head of cattle, many of which are his own, wintering up here, and makes no end of money by taking in people at eight dollars a week, yet it all goes somehow.

He has a most industrious wife, a girl of seventeen, and four younger children, all musical, but the wife has to work like a slave; and though he is a kind husband, her lot, as compared with her lord's, is like that of a squaw. Edwards, his partner, is his exact opposite, tall, thin, and condemnatory-looking, keen, industrious, saving, grave, a teetotaller, grieved for all reasons at Evans's follies, and rather grudging; as naturally unpopular as Evans is popular; a 'decent man,' who, with his industrious wife, will certainly make money as fast as Evans loses it.

I pay eight dollars a week, which includes the unlimited use of a horse, when one can be found and caught. We breakfast at seven on beef, potatoes, tea, coffee, new bread, and butter. Two pitchers of cream and two of milk are replenished as fast as they are exhausted. Dinner at twelve is a repetition of the breakfast, but with the coffee omitted and a gigantic pudding added. Tea at six is a repetition of breakfast. 'Eat whenever you are hungry, you can always get milk and bread in the kitchen,' Evans says – 'eat as much as you can, it'll do you good,' and we all eat like hunters. There is no change of food. The steer which was being killed on my arrival is now being eaten through from head to tail, the meat being hacked off quite promiscuously, without any regard to joints. In this dry, rarefied air, the outside of the flesh blackens and hardens, and though the weather may be hot, the carcass keeps sweet for two or three months. The bread is super-excellent, but the poor wives seem to be making and baking it all day.

The regular household living and eating together at this time consists of a very intelligent and high-minded American couple, Mr and Mrs Dewy, people whose character, culture, and society I should value anywhere; a young Englishman, brother of a celebrated African traveller, who, because he rides on an English saddle, and clings to some other insular peculiarities, is called 'The Earl;' a miner prospecting for silver; a young man, the type of intelligent, practical 'Young America,' whose health showed consumptive tendencies when he was in business, and who is living a hunter's life here; a grown-up niece of Evans; and a melancholy-looking hired man. A mile off there is an industrious married settler, and four miles off, in the gulch leading to the Park, 'Mountain Jim,' otherwise Mr Nugent, is posted. His business as a trapper takes him daily up to the beaver-dams in Black Canyon to look after his traps, and he generally spends some time in or about our cabin, not, I can see, to Evans's satisfaction. For, in truth, this blue hollow, lying solitary at the foot of Long's Peak, is a miniature world of great interest, in which love, jealousy, hatred, envy, pride, unselfishness, greed, selfishness, and self-sacrifice can be studied hourly, and there is always the unpleasantly exciting risk of an open quarrel with the neighbouring desperado, whose 'I'll shoot you!' has more than once been heard in the cabin.

The party, however, has often been increased by 'campers,' either elk hunters or 'prospectors' for silver or locations, who feed with us and join us in the evening. They get little help from Evans, either as to elk or locations, and go away disgusted and unsuccessful. Two Englishmen of refinement and culture camped out here prospecting a few weeks ago, and then, contrary to advice, crossed the mountains into North Park, where gold is said to abound, and it is believed that they have fallen victims to the bloodthirsty Indians of that region. Of course, we never get letters or newspapers unless some one rides to Longmount for them. Two or three novels and a copy of *Our New West* are our literature. Our latest newspaper is seventeen days old. Somehow the Park seems to become the natural limit of our interests so far as they appear in conversation at table. The last grand aurora, the prospect of a snowstorm, track and sign of elk and grizzly, rumours of a big-horn herd near the lake, the canyons in which the Texan cattle were last seen, the merits of different rifles, the progress of two obvious love affairs, the probability of some one coming up from the Plains with letters, 'Mountain Jim's' latest mood or escapade, and the merits of his dog 'Ring' as compared with those of Evans's dog 'Plunk,' are among the topics which are never abandoned as exhausted.

On Sunday work is nominally laid aside, but most of the men go out hunting or fishing till the evening, when we have the harmonium and much sacred music and singing in parts. To be alone in the Park from the afternoon till the last glory of the afterglow has faded, with no books but a Bible and Prayer-book, is truly delightful. No worthier temple for a 'Te Deum' or 'Gloria in Excelsis' could be found than this 'temple not made with hands,' in which one may worship without being distracted by the sight of bonnets of endless form, and curiously intricate 'back hair,' and countless oddities of changing fashion.

I shall not soon forget my first night here.

Somewhat dazed by the rarefied air, entranced by the glorious beauty, slightly puzzled by the motley company, whose faces loomed not always quite distinctly through the cloud of smoke produced by eleven pipes, I went to my solitary cabin at nine, attended by Evans. It was very dark, and it seemed a long way off. Something howled – Evans said it was a wolf – and owls apparently innumerable hooted incessantly. The pole-star, exactly opposite my cabin door, burned like a lamp. The frost was sharp. Evans opened the door, lighted a candle, and left me, and I was soon in my hay bed. I was frightened – that is, afraid of being frightened, it was so eerie; but sleep soon got the better of my fears. I was awoke by a heavy breathing, a noise something like sawing under the floor, and a pushing and upheaving, all very loud. My candle was all burned, and, in truth, I dared not stir. The noise went on for an hour fully, when, just as I thought the floor had been made sufficiently thin for all purposes of ingress, the sounds abruptly ceased, and I fell asleep again. My hair was not, as it ought to have been, white in the morning!

I was dressed by seven, our breakfast-hour, and when I reached the great cabin and told my story, Evans laughed hilariously, and Edwards contorted his face dismally. They told me that there was a skunk's lair under my cabin, and that they dare not make any attempt to dislodge him for fear of rendering the cabin untenable. They have tried to trap him since, but without success, and each night the noisy performance is repeated. I think he is sharpening his claws on the under side of my floor, as the grizzlies sharpen theirs upon the trees. The odour with which this creature, truly named Mephitis, can overpower its assailants is truly *awful*. We were driven out of the cabin for some hours merely by the passage of one across the *corral*. The bravest man is a coward in its neighbourhood. Dogs rub their noses on the ground till they bleed when they have touched the fluid, and even die of the vomiting produced by the effluvia. The odour can be smelt a mile off. If clothes are touched by the fluid they must be destroyed. At present its fur is very valuable. Several have been killed since I came. A shot well aimed at the spine secures one safely, and an experienced dog can kill one by leaping upon it suddenly without being exposed to danger. It is a beautiful beast, about the size and length of a fox, with long thick black or dark-brown fur, and two white streaks from the head to the long bushy tail. The claws of its forefeet are long and polished. Yesterday one was seen rushing from the dairy and was shot. 'Plunk,' the big dog, touched it, and has to be driven into exile. The body was valiantly removed by a man with a long fork, and carried to a running stream, but we are nearly choked with the odour from the spot where it fell. I hope that my skunk will enjoy a quiet spirit so long as we are near neighbours.

[. . .]

October 9

The letter and newspaper fever has seized on every one. We have sent at last to Longmount. This evening I rode out on the Longmount trail towards dusk, escorted by 'Mountain Jim,' and in the distance we saw a waggon with four horses and a saddle-horse behind, and the driver waved a handkerchief, the concerted signal if I were the possessor of a horse. We turned back, galloping down the long hill as fast as two good horses could carry us, and gave the joyful news. It was an hour before the waggon arrived, bringing not Evans but two 'campers' of suspicious aspect, who have pitched their camp close to my cabin! You cannot imagine what it is to be locked in by these mountain walls, and not to know where your letters are lying. Later on, Mr Buchan, one of our usual inmates, returned from Denver with papers, letters for every one but me, and much exciting news. The financial panic has spread out West, gathering strength on its way. The Denver banks have all suspended business. They refuse to cash their own cheques, or to allow their customers to draw a dollar, and would not even give greenbacks for my English gold! Neither Mr Buchan nor Evans could get a cent. Business is suspended, and every body, however rich, is for the time being poor. The Indians have taken to the 'war path,' and are burning ranches and killing cattle. There is a regular 'scare' among the settlers, and waggon loads of fugitives are arriving in Colorado Springs. The Indians say, 'The white man has killed the buffalo and left them to rot on the plains. We will be revenged.' Evans had reached Longmount, and will be here to-night.

October 10

'Wait for the waggon' still! We had a hurricane of wind and hail last night; it was eleven before I could go to my cabin, and I only reached it with the help of two men. The moon was not up, and the sky overhead was black with clouds, when suddenly Long's Peak, which had been invisible, gleamed above the dark mountains, all glistening with new-fallen snow, on which the moon, as yet unrisen here, was shining. The evening before, after sunset, I saw another novel effect. My lake turned a brilliant orange in the twilight, and in its still mirror the mountains were reflected a deep rich blue. It is a world of wonders. To-day we had a great storm with flurries of fine snow; and when the clouds rolled up at noon, the Snowy Range and all the higher mountains were pure white. I have been hard at work all day to drown my anxieties, which are heightened by a rumour that Evans has gone buffalo-hunting on the Platte!

This evening, quite unexpectedly, Evans arrived with a heavy mail in a box. I sorted it, but there was nothing for me, and Evans said he was afraid that he had left my letters, which were separate from the others, behind at Denver, but he had written from Longmount for them. A few hours later they were found in a box of groceries!

All the hilarity of the house has returned with Evans, and he has brought a kindred spirit with him, a young man who plays and sings splendidly, has an inexhaustible *repertoire*, and produces sonatas, funeral marches, anthems, reels, strathspeys, and all else, out of his wonderful memory. Never, surely, was a chamber organ compelled to such service. A little cask of suspicious appearance was smuggled into the cabin from the waggon, and heightens the hilarity a little, I fear. No churlishness could resist Evans's unutterable jollity or the contagion of his hearty laugh. He claps people on the back, shouts at them, will do anything for them, and makes a perpetual breeze. 'My kingdom for a horse!' he has not got one for me, and a shadow crossed his face when I spoke of the subject. Eventually he asked for a private conference, when he told me, with some confusion, that he had found himself 'very hard up' in Denver, and had been obliged to appropriate my 100-dollar note. He said he would give me, as interest for it up to November 25th, a good horse, saddle, and bridle for my proposed journey of 600 miles. I was somewhat dismayed, but there was no other course, as the money was gone. I tried a horse, mended my clothes, reduced my pack to a weight of twelve pounds, and was all ready for an early start, when before daylight I was wakened by Evans's cheery voice at my door. 'I say, Miss B., we've got to drive wild cattle to-day; I wish you'd lend a hand, there's not enough of us; I'll give you a good horse; one day won't make much difference.' So we've been driving cattle all day, riding about twenty miles, and fording the big

Thompson about as many times. Evans flatters me by saying that I am 'as much use as another man;' more than one of our party, I hope, who always avoided the 'ugly' cows.

October 12

I am still here, helping in the kitchen, driving cattle, and riding four or five times a day. Evans detains me each morning by saying, 'Here's lots of horses for you to try,' and after trying five or six a day, I do not find one to my liking. To-day, as I was cantering a tall well-bred one round the lake, he threw the bridle off by a toss of his head, leaving me with the reins in my hands; one bucked, and two have tender feet, and tumbled down. Such are some of our little varieties. Still I hope to get off on my tour in a day or two, so at least as to be able to compare Estes Park with some of the better-known parts of Colorado.

Letter IX

Estes Park, Colorado

Shall I ever get away? We were to have had a grand cattle-hunt yesterday, beginning at 6.30, but the horses were all lost. Often out of fifty horses all that are worth anything are marauding, and a day is lost in hunting for them in the canyons. However, before daylight this morning Evans called through my door, 'Miss Bird, I say, we've got to drive cattle fifteen miles, I wish you'd lend a hand; there's not enough of us; I'll give you a good horse.'

The scene of the drive is at a height of 7500 feet, watered by two rapid rivers. On all sides mountains rise to an altitude of from 11,000 to 15,000 feet, their skirts shaggy with pitch-pine forests, and scarred by deep canyons, wooded and boulder-strewn, opening upon the mountain pasture previously mentioned. Two thousand head of half-wild Texan cattle are scattered in herds throughout the canyons, living on more or less suspicious terms with grizzly and brown bears, mountain lions, elk, mountain sheep, spotted deer, wolves, lynxes, wild cats, beavers, minks, skunks, chipmonks, eagles, rattlesnakes, and all the other two-legged, four-legged, vertebrate and invertebrate inhabitants of this lonely and romantic region. On the whole, they show a tendency rather to the habits of wild than of domestic cattle. They march to water in Indian file, with the bulls leading, and when threatened, take strategic advantage of ridgy ground, slinking warily along in the hollows, the bulls acting as sentinels, and bringing up the rear in case of an attack from dogs. Cows have to be regularly broken-in for milking, being as wild as buffaloes in their unbroken state; but, owing to the comparative dryness of the grasses, and the system of allowing the calf to have the milk during the daytime, a dairy of 200 cows does not produce as much butter as a Devonshire dairy of fifty. Some 'necessary' cruelty is involved in the stockman's business, however humane he may be. The system is one of terrorism, and from the time that the calf is bullied into the branding-pen, and the hot iron burns into his shrinking flesh, to the day when the fatted ox is driven down from his boundless pastures to be slaughtered in Chicago, 'the fear and dread of man' are upon him.

The herds are apt to penetrate the savage canyons which come down from the Snowy Range, when they incur a risk of being snowed up and starved, and it is necessary now and then to hunt them out and drive them down to the 'park.' On this occasion, the whole were driven down for a muster, and for the purpose of branding the calves.

After a 6.30 breakfast this morning, we started, the party being composed of my host, a hunter from the Snowy Range, two stockmen from the Plains, one of whom rode a violent buck-jumper, and was said by his comrade to be the 'best rider in North Americay,' and myself. We were all mounted on Mexican saddles, rode, as the custom is, with light snaffle bridles, leather guards over our feet, and broad wooden stirrups, and each carried his lunch in a pouch slung on the lassoing horn of his saddle. Four big, badly-trained dogs accompanied us. It was a ride of nearly thirty miles, and of many hours, one of the most splendid I ever took. We never got off our horses except to tighten the girths, we ate our lunch with our bridles knotted over our saddle-horns, started over the level at full gallop, leapt over trunks of trees, dashed madly down hillsides rugged with rocks or strewn with great stones, forded deep, rapid streams, saw lovely lakes and views of surpassing magnificence, startled a herd of elk with uncouth heads and monstrous antlers, and in the chase, which for some time was unsuccessful, rode to the very base of Long's Peak, over 14,000 feet high, where the bright waters of one of the affluents of the Platte burst from the eternal snows through a canyon of indescribable majesty. The sun was hot, but at a height of over 8000 feet the air was crisp and frosty, and the enjoyment of riding a good horse under such exhilarating circumstances was extreme. In one wild part of the ride we had to come down a steep hill, thickly wooded with pitch-pines, to leap over the fallen timber, and steer between the dead and living trees to avoid being 'snagged,' or bringing down a heavy dead branch by an unwary touch.

Emerging from this, we caught sight of a thousand Texan cattle feeding in a valley below. The leaders scented us, and, taking fright, began to move off in the direction of the open 'park,' while we were about a mile from and above them. 'Head them off, boys!' our leader shouted; 'all aboard; hark away!' and with something of the 'High, tally-ho in the morning!' away we all went at a hand-gallop down-hill. I could not hold my excited animal; down-hill, up-hill, leaping over rocks and timber, faster every moment the pace grew, and still the leader shouted, 'Go it, boys!' and the horses dashed on at racing speed, passing and repassing each other, till my small but beautiful bay was keeping pace with the immense strides of the great buck-jumper ridden by 'the finest rider in North Americay,' and I was dizzied and breathless by the pace at which we were going. A shorter time than it takes to tell it brought us close to and abreast of the surge of cattle. The bovine waves were a grand sight: huge bulls, shaped like buffaloes, bellowed and roared, and with great oxen and cows with yearling calves, galloped like racers, and we galloped alongside of them, and shortly headed them, and in no time were placed as sentinels across the mouth of the valley. It seemed like infantry awaiting the shock of cavalry as we stood as still as our excited horses would allow. I almost quailed as the surge came on, but when it got close to us my comrades hooted fearfully, and we dashed forward with the dogs, and, with bellowing, roaring, and thunder of hoofs, the wave receded as it came. I rode up to our leader, who received me with much laughter. He said I was 'a good cattleman,' and that he had forgotten that a lady was of the party till he saw me 'come leaping over the timber, and driving with the others.'

It was not for two hours after this that the real business of driving began, and I was obliged to change my thoroughbred for a well-trained cattle-horse – a *broncho*, which could double like a hare, and go over any ground. I had not expected to work like a *vachero*, but so it was, and my Hawaiian experience was very useful. We hunted the various canyons and known 'camps,' driving the herds out of them; and, until we had secured 850 head in the *corral* some hours afterwards, we scarcely saw each other to speak to. Our first difficulty was with a herd which got into some swampy ground, when a cow, which afterwards gave me an infinity of trouble, remained at bay for nearly an hour, tossing the dog three times, and resisting all efforts to dislodge her. She had a large yearling calf with her, and Evans told me that the attachment of a cow to her first calf is sometimes so great that she will kill her second that the first may have the milk. I got a herd of over a hundred out of a canyon by myself, and drove them down to the river with the aid of one badly-broken dog, which gave me more trouble than the cattle. The getting over was most troublesome; a few took to the water readily and went across, but others smelt it, and then, doubling back, ran in various directions; while some attacked the dog as he was swimming, and others, after crossing, headed back in search of some favourite companions which had been left behind, and one specially vicious cow attacked my horse over and over again. It took an hour and a half of time and much patience to gather them all on the other side.

It was getting late in the day, and a snowstorm was impending, before I was joined by the other drivers and herds, and as the former had diminished to three, with only three dogs, it was very difficult to keep the cattle together. You drive them as gently as possible, so as not to frighten or excite them, riding first on one side, then on the other, to guide them; and if they deliberately go in a wrong direction, you gallop in front and head them off. The great excitement is when one breaks away from the herd and gallops madly up and down hill, and you gallop after him anywhere, over and among rocks and trees, doubling when he doubles, and heading him till you get him back again. The bulls were quite easily managed, but the cows with calves, old or young, were most troublesome. By accident I rode between one cow and her calf in a narrow place, and the cow rushed at me and was just getting her big horns under the horse, when he reared, and spun dexterously aside. This kind of thing happened continually. There was one very handsome red cow which became quite mad. She had a calf with her nearly her own size, and thought every one its enemy, and though its horns were well developed, and it was quite able to take care of itself, she insisted on protecting it from all fancied dangers. One of the dogs, a young, foolish thing, seeing that the cow was excited, took a foolish pleasure in barking at her, and she was eventually quite infuriated. She turned to bay forty times at least; tore up the ground with her horns, tossed the great hunting dogs, tossed and killed the calves of two other cows, and finally became so dangerous to the rest of the herd that, just as the drive was ending, Evans drew his revolver and shot her, and the calf for which she had fought so blindly lamented her piteously. She rushed at me several times mad with rage, but these trained cattle-horses keep perfectly cool, and, nearly without will on my part, mine jumped aside at the right moment, and foiled the assailant. Just at dusk we reached the *corral* – an acre of grass enclosed by stout post-and-rail fences seven feet high, and by much patience and some subtlety lodged the whole herd within its shelter, without a blow, a shout, or even a crack of a whip, wild as the cattle were. It was fearfully cold. We galloped the last mile and a half in four and a half minutes, reached the cabin just as snow began to fall, and found strong, hot tea ready.

October 18

Snow-bound for three days! I could not write yesterday, it was so awful. People gave up all occupation, and talked of nothing but the storm. The hunters all kept by the great fire in the living-room, only going out to bring in logs and clear the snow from the door and windows. I never spent a more fearful night than two nights ago, alone in my cabin in the storm, with the roof lifting, the mud cracking and coming off, and the fine snow hissing through the chinks between the logs, while splittings and breaking of dead branches, wind-wrung and snow-laden, went on incessantly, with screechings, howlings, thunder and lightning, and many unfamiliar sounds besides. After snowing fiercely all day, another foot of it fell in the early night, and, after drifting against my door, blocked me effectually in. About midnight the mercury fell to zero, and soon after a gale rose, which lasted for ten hours. My window frame is swelled, and shuts, apparently, hermetically, and my bed is six feet from it. I had gone to sleep with six blankets on, and a heavy sheet over my face. Between two and three I was awoke by the cabin being shifted from underneath by the wind, and the sheet was frozen to my lips. I put out my hands, and the bed was thickly covered with fine snow. Getting up to investigate matters, I found the floor some inches deep in parts in fine snow, and a gust of fine, needle-like snow stung my face. The bucket of water was solid ice. I lay in bed freezing till sunrise, when some of the men came to see if I 'was alive,' and to dig me out. They brought a can of hot water, which turned to ice before I could use it. I dressed standing in snow, and my brushes, boots, and etceteras were covered with snow. When I ran to the house, not a mountain or anything else could be seen, and the snow on one side was drifted higher than the roof. The air, as high as one could see, was one white, stinging smoke of snow-drift – a terrific sight. In the living-room, the snow was driving through the chinks, and Mrs Dewy was shovelling it from the floor. Mr D.'s beard was hoary with frost in a room with a fire all night. Evans was lying ill, with his bed covered with snow. Returning from my cabin after breakfast, loaded with occupations for the day, I was lifted off my feet, and deposited in a drift, and all my things, writing-book and letter included, were carried in different directions. Some, including a valuable photograph, are irrecoverable. The writing-book was found, some hours afterwards, under three feet of snow.

There are tracks of bears and deer close to the house, but no one can hunt in this gale, and the drift is blinding. We have been slightly overcrowded in our one room. Chess, music, and whist have been resorted to. One hunter, for very *ennui*, has devoted himself to keeping my ink from freezing. We all sat in great cloaks and coats, and kept up an enormous fire, with the pitch running out of the logs. The isolation is extreme, for we are literally snowed-up, and the other settler in the Park and 'Mountain Jim' are both at Denver. Late in the evening the storm ceased. In some places the ground is bare of snow, while in others all irregularities are levelled, and the drifts are forty feet deep. Nature is grand under this new aspect. The cold is awful; the high wind with the mercury at zero would skin any part exposed to it.

October 19

South Park is closed, or nearly so, by snow during an ordinary winter; and just now the great freight waggons are carrying up the last supplies of the season, and taking down women and other temporary inhabitants. A great many people come up here in the summer. The rarefied air produces great oppression on the lungs, accompanied with bleeding. It is said that you can tell a new arrival by seeing him go about holding a blood-stained handkerchief to his mouth. But I came down upon it from regions of ice and snow; and as the snow which had fallen on it had all disappeared by evaporation and drifting, it looked to me quite lowland and livable, though lonely and indescribably mournful, 'a silent sea,' suggestive of 'the muffled oar.' I cantered across the narrow end of it, delighted to have got through the snow; and when I struck the 'Denver stage-road' I supposed that all the difficulties of mountain travel were at an end, but this has not turned out to be exactly the case.

A horseman shortly joined me and rode with me, got me a fresh horse, and accompanied me for ten miles. He was a picturesque figure and rode a very good horse. He wore a big slouch hat, from under which a number of fair curls hung nearly to his waist. His beard was fair, his eyes blue, and his complexion ruddy. There was nothing sinister in his expression, and his manner was respectful and frank. He was dressed in a hunter's buckskin suit ornamented with beads, and wore a pair of exceptionally big brass spurs. His saddle was very highly ornamented. What was unusual was the number of weapons he carried. Besides a rifle laid across his saddle and a pair of pistols in the holsters, he carried two revolvers and a knife in his belt, and a carbine slung behind him. I found him what is termed 'good company.' He told me a great deal about the country and its wild animals, with some hunting adventures, and a great deal about Indians and their cruelty and treachery. All this time, having crossed South Park, we were ascending the Continental Divide by what I think is termed the Breckenridge Pass, on a fairly good waggon-road. We stopped at a cabin, where the woman seemed to know my companion, and, in addition to bread and milk, produced some venison steaks. We rode on again, and reached the crest of the Divide and saw snow-born streams starting within a quarter of a mile from each other, one for the Colorado and the Pacific, the other for the Platte and the Atlantic. Here I wished the hunter good-bye, and reluctantly turned north-east. It was not wise to go up the Divide at all, and it was necessary to do it in haste. On my way down I spoke to the woman at whose cabin I had dined, and she said, 'I am sure you found Comanche Bill a real gentleman;' and I then knew that, if she gave me correct information, my intelligent, courteous companion was one of the most notorious desperadoes of the Rocky Mountains, and the greatest Indian exterminator on the frontier – a man whose father and family fell in a massacre at Spirit Lake by the hands of Indians, who carried away his sister, then a child of eleven. His life has since been mainly devoted to a search for this child, and to killing Indians wherever he can find them.

[. . .]

The Americans will never solve the Indian problem till the Indian is extinct. They have treated them after a fashion which has intensified their treachery and 'devilry' as enemies, and as friends reduces them to a degraded pauperism, devoid of the very first elements of civilisation. The only difference between the savage and the civilised Indian is that the latter carries firearms and gets drunk on whisky. The Indian Agency has been a sink of fraud and corruption; it is said that barely thirty per cent of the allowance ever reaches those for whom it is voted; and the complaints of shoddy blankets, damaged flour, and worthless firearms are universal. 'To get rid of the Injuns' is the phrase used everywhere. Even their 'reservations' do not escape seizure practically; for if gold 'breaks out' on them they are 'rushed,' and their possessors are either compelled to accept land farther west or are shot off and driven off. One of the surest agents in their destruction is vitriolised whisky. An attempt has recently been made to cleanse the Augean stable of the Indian Department, but it has met with signal failure, the usual result in America of every effort to purify the official atmosphere. Americans specially love superlatives. The phrases 'biggest in the world,' 'finest in the world,' are on all lips. Unless the President is a strong man they will soon come to boast that their government is composed of the 'biggest scoundrels' in the world.

[. . .]

I never told you that I once gave an unwary promise that I would not travel alone in Colorado unarmed, and that in consequence I left Estes Park with a Sharp's revolver loaded with ball-cartridge in my pocket, which has been the plague of my life. Its bright ominous barrel peeped out in quiet Denver shops, children pulled it out to play with, or when my riding-dress hung up with it in the pocket, pulled the whole from the peg to the floor; and I cannot conceive of any circumstances in which I could feel it right to make any use of it, or in which it could do me any possible good. Last night, however, I took it out, cleaned and oiled it, and laid it under my pillow, resolving to keep awake all night. I slept as soon as I lay down, and never woke till the bright morning sun shone through the roof, making me ridicule my own fears and abjure pistols for ever!

[. . .]

When I left Golden City it was a brilliant summer afternoon, and not too hot. They could not give any directions at the stable, and told me to go out on the Denver track till I met some one who could direct me, which started me off wrong from the first. After riding about two miles I met a man who told me I was all wrong, and directed me across the prairie till I met another, who gave me so many directions that I forgot them, and was irretrievably lost. The afterglow, seen to perfection on the open plain, was wonderful. Just as it grew dark I rode after a teamster who said I was then four miles farther from Boulder than when I left Golden, and directed me to a house seven miles off. I suppose he thought I should know, for he told me to cross the prairie till I came to a place where three tracks are seen, and there to take the best-travelled one, steering all the time by the north star. His directions did bring me to tracks, but it was then so dark that I could see nothing, and soon became so dark that I could not even see Birdie's ears, and was lost and benighted. I rode on, hour after hour, in the darkness and solitude, the prairie all round and a firmament of frosty stars overhead. The prairie wolf howled now and then, and occasionally the lowing of cattle gave me hope of human proximity. But there was nothing but the lone wild plain. You can hardly imagine the longing to see a light, to hear a voice, the intensely eerie feeling of being alone in that vast solitude. It was freezing very sharply and was very cold, and I was making up my mind to steer all night for the Pole Star, much fearing that I should be brought up by one of the affluents of the Platte, or that Birdie would tire, when I heard the undertoned bellowing of a bull, which, from the snorting and rooting up of earth, seemed to be disputing the right of way, and the pony was afraid to pass. While she was scuffling about, I heard a dog bark and a man swear; then I saw a light, and in another minute found myself at a large house, where I knew the people, only eleven miles from Denver! It was nearly midnight, and light, warmth, and a good bed were truly welcome.

You can form no idea of what the glory on the plains is just before sunrise. Like the afterglow, for a great height above the horizon there is a shaded band of the most intense and glowing orange, while the mountains which reflect the yet unrisen sun have the purple light of amethysts. I left early, but soon lost the track and was lost; but knowing that a sublime gash in the mountains was Bear Canyon, quite near Boulder, I struck across the prairie for it, and then found the Boulder track. 'The best-laid schemes of men and mice gang aft agee,' and my exploits came to an untimely end to-day. On arriving here, instead of going into the mountains, I was obliged to go to bed in consequence of vertigo, headache, and faintness, produced by the intense heat of the sun. In all that weary land there was no 'shadow of a great rock' under which to rest. The gravelly, baked soil reflected the fiery sun, and it was nearly maddening to look up at the cool blue of the mountains, with their stretches of pines and their deep indigo shadows. Boulder is a hideous collection of frame houses on the burning plain, but it aspires to be a 'city' in virtue of being a 'distributing point' for the settlements up the Boulder Canyon, and of the discovery of a coal-seam.

Longmount, November

I got up very early this morning, and on a hired horse went nine miles up the Boulder Canyon, which is much extolled, but I was greatly disappointed with everything except its superb waggon-road, and much disgusted with the laziness of the horse. A ride of fifteen miles across the prairie brought me here early in the afternoon, but of the budget of letters which I expected there is not one. Birdie looks in such capital condition that my host here can hardly believe that she has travelled over 500 miles. I am feeling 'the pinch of poverty' rather severely. When I have paid my bill here I shall have exactly twenty-six cents left. Evans was quite unable to pay the hundred dollars which he owes me, and, to save themselves, the Denver banks, though they remain open, have suspended payment, and would not cash my circular notes. The financial straits are very serious, and the unreasoning panic which has set in makes them worse. The present state of matters is – nobody has any money, so nothing is worth anything. The result to me is that, *nolens volens*, I must go up to Estes Park, where I can live without ready money, and remain there till things change for the better. It does not seem a very hard fate! Long's Peak rises in purple gloom, and I long for the cool air and unfettered life of the solitary blue hollow at its base.

[. . .]

Letter XIV

Estes Park

Mr Nugent came in looking very black, and asked me to ride with him to see the beaver dams on the Black Canyon. No more whistling or singing, or talking to his beautiful mare, or sparkling repartee. His mood was as dark as the sky overhead, which was black with an impending snowstorm. He was quite silent, struck his horse often, started off on a furious gallop, and then throwing his mare on her haunches close to me, said, 'You're the first man or woman who's treated me like a human being for many a year.' So he said in this dark mood, but Mr and Mrs Dewy, who took a very deep interest in his welfare, always treated him as a rational, intelligent gentleman, and in his better moments he spoke of them with the warmest appreciation. 'If you want to know,' he continued, 'how nearly a man can become a devil, I'll tell you now.' There was no choice, and we rode up the canyon, and I listened to one of the darkest tales of ruin I have ever heard or read. Its early features were very simple. His father was a British officer quartered at Montreal, of a good old Irish family. From his account he was an ungovernable boy, imperfectly educated, and tyrannising over a loving but weak mother. When seventeen years old he saw a young girl at church whose appearance he described as being of angelic beauty, and fell in love with her with all the intensity of an uncontrolled nature. He saw her three times, but scarcely spoke to her. On his mother opposing his wish and treating it as a boyish folly, he took to drink 'to spite her,' and almost as soon as he was eighteen, maddened by the girl's death, he ran away from home, entered the service of the Hudson's Bay Company, and remained in it for several years, only leaving it because he found even that lawless life too strict for him. Then, being as I suppose about twenty-seven, he entered the service of the United States Government, and became one of the famous Indian Scouts of the Plains, distinguishing himself by some of the most daring deeds on record, and some of the bloodiest crimes. Some of these tales I have heard before, but never so terribly told. Years must have passed in that service, till he became a character known through all the West, and much dreaded for his readiness to take offence, and his equal readiness with his revolver. Vain, even in his dark mood, he told me that he was idolised by women, and that in his worst hours he was always chivalrous to good women. He described himself as riding through camps in his scout's dress with a red scarf round his waist, and sixteen golden curls, eighteen inches long, hanging over his shoulders. The handsome, even superbly handsome, side of his face was towards me as he spoke. As a scout and as an armed escort of emigrant parties he was evidently implicated in all the blood and broil of a lawless region and period, and went from bad to worse, varying his life by drunken sprees, which brought nothing but violence and loss. The narrative seemed to lack some link, for I next found him on a homestead in Missouri, from whence he came to Colorado a few years ago. There, again, something was dropped out, but I suspect, and not without reason, that he joined one or more of those gangs of 'border ruffians' which for so long raided through Kansas, perpetrating such massacres and outrages as that of the Marais du Cygne. His fame for violence and ruffianism preceded him into Colorado, where his knowledge of and love of the mountains have earned him the *sobriquet* he now bears. He has a squatter's claim and forty head of cattle, and is a successful trapper besides, but envy and vindictiveness are raging within him. He gets money, goes to Denver, and spends large sums in the maddest dissipation, making himself a terror, and going beyond even such desperadoes as 'Texas Jack' and 'Wild Bill;' and when the money is done returns to his mountain den, full of hatred and self-scorn, till the next time. Of course I cannot give details. The story took three hours to tell, and was crowded with terrific illustrations of a desperado's career, told with a rush of wild eloquence that was truly thrilling. When the snow, which for some time had been falling, compelled him to break off and guide me to a sheltered place from which I could make my own way back again, he stopped his horse and said, 'Now you see a man who has made a devil of himself! Lost! Lost! Lost! I believe in God. I've given Him no choice but to put me with "the devil and his angels." I'm afraid to die. You've stirred the better nature in me too late. I can't change. If ever a man were a slave, I am. Don't speak to me of repentance and reformation. I can't reform. Your voice reminded me of –.' Then in feverish tones, 'How dare you ride with me? You won't speak to me again, will you?' He made me promise to keep one or two things secret whether he were living or dead, and I promised, for I had no choice; but they come between me and the sunshine sometimes, and I wake at night to think of them. I wish I had been spared the regret and excitement of that afternoon. A less ungovernable nature would never have spoken as he did, nor told me what he did; but his proud, fierce soul all poured itself out then, with hatred and self-loathing, blood on his hands and murder in his heart, though even then he could not be altogether other than a gentleman, or altogether divest himself of fascination, even when so tempestuously revealing the darkest points of his character. My soul dissolved in pity for his dark, lost, self-ruined life, as he left me and turned away in the blinding storm to the Snowy Range, where he said he was going to camp out for a fortnight; a man of great abilities, real genius, singular gifts, and with all the chances in life which other men have had. How far more terrible than the '*Actum est: periisti*' of Cowper is his exclamation, 'Lost! Lost! Lost!'

[. . .]

The Fall river has had its source completely altered by the operations of the beavers. Their engineering skill is wonderful. In one place they have made a lake by damming up the stream; in another their works have created an island, and they have made several falls. Their storehouses, of course, are carefully concealed. By this time they are about full for the winter. We saw quantities of young cotton-wood and aspen-trees, with stems about as thick as my arm, lying where these industrious creatures have felled them ready for their use. They always work at night and in concert. Their long, sharp teeth are used for gnawing down the trees, but their mason-work is done entirely with their flat, trowel-like tails. In its natural state the fur is very durable, and is as full of long black hairs as that of the sable, but as sold, all these hairs have been plucked out of it.

Letter XV

Estes Park, Sunday

A trapper passing last night brought us the news that Mr Nugent is ill; so, after washing up the things after our late breakfast, I rode to his cabin, but I met him in the gulch coming down to see us. He said he had caught cold on the Range, and was suffering from an old arrow wound in the lung. We had a long conversation without adverting to the former one, and he told me some of the present circumstances of his ruined life. It is piteous that a man like him, in the prime of life, should be destitute of home and love, and live a life of darkness in a den with no companions but guilty memories, and a dog which many people think is the nobler animal of the two. I urged him to give up the whisky which at present is his ruin, and his answer had the ring of a sad truth in it: 'I cannot, it binds me hand and foot – I cannot give up the only pleasure I have.' His ideas of right are the queerest possible. He says that he believes in God, but what he knows or believes of God's law I know not. To resent insult with your revolver, to revenge yourself on those who have injured you, to be true to a comrade and share your last crust with him, to be chivalrous to good women, to be generous and hospitable, and at the last to die game –

these are the articles of his creed, and I suppose they are received by men of his stamp. He hates Evans with a bitter hatred, and Evans returns it, having undergone much provocation from Jim in his moods of lawlessness and violence, and being not a little envious of the fascination which his manners and conversation have for the strangers who come up here.

On returning down the gulch the view was grander than I have ever seen it, the gulch in dark shadow, the Park below lying in intense sunlight, with all the majestic canyons which sweep down upon it in depths of infinite blue gloom, and above, the pearly peaks, dazzling in purity and glorious in form, cleft the turquoise blue of the sky. How shall I ever leave this 'land which is very far off'? How *can* I ever leave it? is the real question. We are going on the principle, 'Let us eat and drink, for to-morrow we die,' and the stores are melting away. The two meals are not an economical plan, for we are so much more hungry that we eat more than when we had three. We had a good deal of sacred music to-day, to make it as like Sunday as possible. The 'faint melancholy' of this winter loneliness is very fascinating. How glorious the amber fires of the winter dawns are, and how gloriously to-night the crimson clouds descended just to the mountain-tops and were reflected on the pure surface of the snow! The door of this room looks due north, and as I write the Pole Star blazes, and a cold crescent moon hangs over the ghastliness of Long's Peak.

Estes Park, Colorado, November

We have lost count of time, and can only agree on the fact that the date is somewhere near the end of November. Our life has settled down into serenity, and our singular and enforced partnership is very pleasant. We might be three men living together, but for the unvarying courtesy and consideration which they show to me. Our work goes on like clockwork; the only difficulty which ever arises is that the men do not like me to do anything that they think hard or unsuitable, such as saddling a horse or bringing in water. The days go very fast; it was 3.30 to-day before I knew that it was 1. It is a calm life without worries. The men are so easy to live with; they never fuss, or grumble, or sigh, or make a trouble of anything. It would amuse you to come into our wretched little kitchen before our disgracefully late breakfast, and find Mr Kavan busy at the stove frying venison, myself washing the supper-dishes, and Mr Buchan drying them, or both the men busy at the stove while I sweep the floor. Our food is a great object of interest to us, and we are ravenously hungry now that we have only two meals a day. About sundown each goes forth to his 'chores' – Mr K. to chop wood, Mr B. to haul water, I to wash the milk-pans and water the horses. On Saturday the men shot a deer, and on going for it to-day they found nothing but the hind legs, and following a track which they expected would lead them to a beast's hole, they came quite carelessly upon a large mountain lion, which, however, took itself out of their reach before they were sufficiently recovered from their surprise to fire at it. These lions, which are really a species of puma, are bloodthirsty as well as cowardly. Lately one got into a sheepfold in the canyon of the St Vrain, and killed thirty sheep, sucking the blood from their throats.

November ?

This has been a day of minor events, as well as a busy one. I was so busy that I never sat down from 10.30 till 1.30. I had washed my one change of raiment, and though I never iron my clothes, I like to bleach them till they are as white as snow, and they were whitening on the line when some furious gusts came down from Long's Peak, against which I could not stand, and when I did get out all my clothes were blown into strips from an inch to four inches in width, literally destroyed! One learns how very little is necessary either for comfort or happiness. I made a four-pound spiced ginger cake, baked some bread, mended my riding dress, cleaned up generally, wrote some letters with the hope that some day they might be posted, and took a magnificent walk, reaching the cabin again in the melancholy glory which now immediately precedes the darkness. We were all busy getting our supper ready when the dogs began to bark furiously, and we heard the noise of horses. 'Evans at last!' we exclaimed, but we were wrong. Mr Kavan went out, and returned saying that it was a young man who had come up with

Evans's waggon and team, and that the waggon had gone over into a gulch seven miles from here. Mr Kavan looked very grave. 'It's another mouth to feed,' he said. They asked no questions, and brought the lad in, a slangy, assured fellow of twenty, who, having fallen into delicate health at a theological college, had been sent up here by Evans to work for his board. The men were too courteous to ask him what he was doing up here, but I boldly asked him where he lived, and to our dismay he replied, 'I've come to live here.' So we had to settle what to do with him. We discussed the food question gravely, as it presented a real difficulty. We put him into a bed-closet opening from the kitchen, and decided to see what he was fit for before giving him work. We were very much amazed, in truth, at his coming here. He is evidently a shallow, arrogant youth.

We have decided that to-day is November 26th; to-morrow is Thanksgiving Day, and we are planning a feast, though Mr K. said to me again this morning with a doleful face, 'You see there's another mouth to feed.' This 'mouth' has come up to try the panacea of manual labour, but he is town-bred, and I see that he will do nothing. He is writing poetry, and while I was busy to-day began to read it aloud to me, asking for my criticism. He is just at the age when everything literary has a fascination, and every literary person is a hero, specially Dr Holland. Last night was fearful from the lifting of the cabin and the breaking of the mud from the roof. We sat with fine gravel driving in our faces, and this morning I carried four shovelfuls of mud out of my room. After breakfast, Mr Kavan, Mr Lyman, and I, with the two waggon-horses, rode the seven miles to the scene of yesterday's disaster in a perfect gale of wind. I felt like a servant going out for a day's 'pleasuring,' hurrying 'through my dishes,' and leaving my room in disorder. The waggon lay half-way down the side of a ravine, kept from destruction by having caught on some trees. It was too cold to hang about while the men hauled it up and fixed it, so I went slowly back, encountering Mr Nugent in a most bitter mood – almost in an 'ugly fit' – hating everybody, and contrasting his own generosity and reckless kindness with the selfishness and carefully-weighed kindnesses of others. People do give him credit for having 'as kind a heart as ever beat.' Lately a child in the other cabin was taken ill, and though there were idle men and horses at hand, it was only the 'desperado' who rode sixty miles in 'the shortest time ever made' to bring the doctor. While we were talking he was sitting on a stone outside his den mending a saddle, skins, bones, and skulls lying about him, 'Ring' watching him with jealous and idolatrous affection, the wind lifting his thin curls from as grand a head as was ever modelled – a ruin of a man. Yet the sun which shines 'on the evil and the good' was lighting up the gold of his hair. May our Father which is in heaven yet show mercy to His outcast child!

Mr Kavan soon overtook me, and we had an exciting race of two miles, getting home just before the wind fell and the snow began.

Thanksgiving Day. The thing dreaded has come at

last, a snowstorm, with a north-east wind. It ceased about midnight, but not till it had covered my bed. Then the mercury fell below zero, and everything froze. I melted a tin of water for washing by the fire, but it was hard frozen before I could use it. My hair, which was thoroughly wet with the thawed snow of yesterday, is hard frozen in plaits. The milk and treacle are like rock, the eggs have to be kept on the coolest part of the stove to keep them fluid. Two calves in the shed were frozen to death. Half our floor is deep in snow, and it is so cold that we cannot open the door to shovel it out. The snow began again at eight this morning, very fine and hard. It blows in through the chinks and dusts this letter while I write. Mr Kavan keeps my ink-bottle close to the fire, and hands it to me every time that I need to dip my pen. We have a huge fire, but cannot raise the temperature above 20°. Ever since I returned the lake has been hard enough to bear a waggon, but to-day it is difficult to keep the water-hole open by the constant use of the axe. The snow may either melt or block us in. Our only anxiety is about the supplies. We have tea and coffee enough to last over to-morrow, the sugar is just done, and the flour is getting low. It is really serious that we have 'another mouth to feed,' and the new-comer is a ravenous creature, eating more than the three of us. It dismays me to see his hungry eyes gauging the supply at breakfast, and to see the loaf disappear. He told me this morning that he could eat the whole of what was on the table. He is mad after food, and I see that Mr K. is starving himself to make it hold out. Mr Buchan is very far from well, and dreads the prospect of 'half rations.' All this sounds laughable, but we shall not laugh if we have to look hunger in the face! Now in the evening the snow-clouds, which have blotted out all things, are lifting, and the winter scene is wonderful. The mercury is 5° below zero, and the aurora is glorious. In my unchinked room the mercury is 1° below zero. Mr Buchan can hardly get his breath; the dryness is intense. We spent the afternoon cooking the Thanksgiving dinner. I made a wonderful pudding, for which I had saved eggs and cream for days, and dried and stoned cherries supplied the place of currants. I made a bowl of custard for sauce, which the men said was 'splendid;' also a rolled pudding, with molasses; and we had venison steaks and potatoes, but for tea we were obliged to use the tea-leaves of the morning again. I should think that few people in America have enjoyed their Thanksgiving dinner more. We had urged Mr Nugent to join us; but he refused, almost savagely, which we regretted. My four-pound cake made yesterday is all gone! This wretched boy confesses that he was so hungry in the night that he got up and ate nearly half of it. He is trying to cajole me into making another.

November 29

Before the boy came I had mistaken some faded cayenne pepper for ginger, and had made a cake with it. Last evening I put half of it into the cupboard and left the door open. During the night we heard a commotion in the kitchen and much choking, coughing, and groaning, and at breakfast the boy was unable to swallow food with his usual ravenousness. After breakfast he came to me whimpering, and asking for something soothing for his throat, admitting that he had seen the 'ginger bread,' and 'felt so starved' in the night that he got up to eat it. I tried to make him feel that it was 'real mean' to eat so much and be so useless, and he said he would do anything to help me, but the men were so 'down on him.' I never saw men so patient with a lad before. He is a most vexing addition to our party, yet one cannot help laughing at him. He is not honourable, though. I dare not leave this letter lying on the table, as he would read it. He writes for two Western periodicals (at least he says so), and he shows us long pieces of his published poetry. In one there are twenty lines copied (as Mr Kavan has shown me) without alteration from *Paradise Lost*; in another there are two stanzas from *Resignation*, with only the alteration of 'stray' for 'dead;' and he has passed the whole of Bonar's *Meeting-place* off as his own. Again, he lent me an essay by himself, called *The Function of the Novelist*, which is nothing but a mosaic of unacknowledged quotations. The men tell me that he has 'bragged' to them that on his way here he took shelter in Mr Nugent's cabin, found out where he hides his key, opened his box, and read his letters and MSS. He is a perfect plague with his ignorance and self-sufficiency. The first day after he came, while I was washing up the breakfast-things, he told me that he intended to do all the dirty work, so I left the knives and forks in the tub and asked him to wipe and lay them aside. Two hours afterwards I found them untouched. Again, the men went out hunting, and he said he would chop the wood for several days' use, and after a few strokes, which were only successful in chipping off some shavings, he came in and strummed on the harmonium, leaving me without any wood with which to make the fire for supper. He talked about his skill with the lasso, but could not even catch one of our quietest horses. Worse than all, he does not know one cow from another. Two days ago he lost our milch cow in driving her in to be milked, and Mr Kavan lost hours of valuable time in hunting for her without success. To-day he told us triumphantly that he had found her, and he was sent out to milk her. After two hours he returned with a rueful face and a few drops of whitish fluid in the milk-pail, saying that that was all he could get. On Mr K. going out, he found, instead of our 'calico' cow, a brindled one that had been dry since the spring! Our cow has gone off to the wild cattle, and we are looking very grim at Lyman, who says that he expected he should live on milk. I told him to fill up the four-gallon kettle, and an hour afterwards found it red-hot on the stove. Nothing can be kept from him unless it is hidden in my room. He has eaten two pounds of dried cherries from the shelf, half of my second four-pound spiced loaf before it was cold, licked up my custard sauce in the night, and privately devoured the pudding which was to be for supper. He confesses to it all, and says, 'I suppose you think me a cure.' Mr K. says that the first thing he said to him this morning was, 'Will Miss B. make us a nice pudding to-day?' This is all harmless, but the plagiarism and want of honour are disgusting, and quite out of keeping with his profession of being a theological student.

This life is in some respects like being on board ship – there are no mails, and one knows nothing beyond one's little world, a very little one in this case. We find each other true, and have learnt to esteem and trust each other. I should, for instance, go out of this room leaving this book open on the table, knowing that the men would not read my letter. They are discreet, reticent, observant, and on many subjects well-informed, but they are of a type which has no antitype at home. All women work in this region, so there is no fuss about my working, or saying, 'Oh, you mustn't do that,' or 'Oh, let me do that.'

November 30

We sat up till eleven last night, so confident were we that Edwards would leave Denver the day after Thanksgiving and get up here. This morning we came to the resolution that we must break up. Tea, coffee, and sugar are done, the venison is turning sour, and the men have only one month left for the hunting on which their winter living depends. I cannot leave the Territory till I get money, but I can go to Longmount for the mail and hear whether the panic is abating. Yesterday I was alone all day, and after riding to the base of Long's Peak, made two roly-poly puddings for supper, having nothing else. The men, however, came back perfectly loaded with trout, and we had a feast. Epicures at home would have envied us. Mr Kavan kept the frying-pan with boiling butter on the stove, butter enough thoroughly to cover the trout, rolled them in coarse corn-meal, plunged them into the butter, turned them once, and took them out, thoroughly done, fizzing, and lemon-coloured. For once young Lyman was satisfied, for the dish was replenished as often as it was emptied. They caught 40 lbs., and have packed them in ice until they can be sent to Denver for sale. The winter fishing is very rich. In the hardest frost, men who fish not for sport, but gain, take their axes and camping blankets, and go up to the hard-frozen waters which lie in fifty places round the Park, and choosing a likely spot, a little sheltered from the wind, hack a hole in the ice, and fastening a foot-link to a cotton-wood tree, bait the hook with maggots or bits of easily-gotten fresh meat. Often the trout are caught as fast as the hook can be baited, and looking through the ice-hole in the track of a sunbeam, you see a mass of tails, silver fins, bright eyes, and crimson spots, a perfect shoal of fish, and truly beautiful the crimson-spotted creatures look, lying still and dead on the blue ice under the sunshine. Sometimes two men bring home 60 lbs. of trout as the result of one day's winter fishing. It is a cold and silent sport, however. How a cook at home would despise our scanty appliances, with which we turn out luxuries. We have only a cooking-stove, which requires incessant feeding with wood, a kettle, a frying-pan, a six-gallon brass pan, and a bottle for a rolling-pin. The cold has been very severe, but I do not suffer from it even in my insufficient clothing. I take a piece of granite made very hot to bed, draw the blankets over my head, and sleep eight hours, though the snow often covers me. One day of snow, mist, and darkness was rather depressing, and yesterday a hurricane began about five in the morning, and the whole Park was one swirl of drifting snow, like stinging wood smoke. My bed and room were white, and the frost was so intense that water brought in a kettle hot from the fire froze as I poured it into the basin. Then the snow ceased, and a fierce wind blew most of it out of the Park, lifting it from the mountains in such clouds as to make Long's Peak look like a smoking volcano. To-day the sky has resumed its delicious blue, and the Park its unrivalled beauty. I have cleaned all the windows, which, ever since I have been here, I supposed were of discoloured glass, so opaque and dirty they were; and when the men came home from fishing they found a cheerful new world. We had a great deal of sacred music and singing on Sunday. Mr Buchan asked me if I knew a tune called 'America,' and began the grand roll of our National Anthem to the words:

'My country, 'tis of thee,
Sweet land of liberty,' etc.

December 1

I was to have started for Canyon to-day, but was awoke by snow as stinging as pinpoints beating on my hand. We all got up early, but it did not improve until nearly noon. In the afternoon Lyman and I rode to Mr Nugent's cabin. I wanted him to read and correct my letter to you, giving the account of our ascent of Long's Peak, but he said he could not, and insisted on our going in, for which young Lyman was more anxious than I was, as Mr Kavan had seen 'Jim' in the morning, and departed from his usual reticence so far as to say, 'There's something wrong with that man; he'll either shoot himself or somebody else.' However, the 'ugly fit' had passed off, and he was so very pleasant and courteous that we remained the whole afternoon. Lyman's one thought was that he could make capital out of the interview, and write an account of the celebrated desperado for a Western paper. The interior of the den was frightful, yet among his black and hideous surroundings the grace of his manner and the genius of his conversation were only more apparent. I read my letter aloud – or rather 'The Ascent of Long's Peak,' which I have written for *Out West* and was sincerely interested with the taste and acumen of his criticisms on the style. He is a true child of nature; his eye brightened and his whole face became radiant, and at last tears rolled down his cheek when I read the account of the glory of the sunrise. Then he read us a very able paper on Spiritualism which he was writing. The den was dense with smoke, and very dark, littered with hay, old blankets, skins, bones, tins, logs, powder-flasks, magazines, old books, old moccasins, horseshoes, and relics of all kinds. He had no better seat to offer me than a log, but offered it with a graceful unconsciousness that it was anything less luxurious than an easy-chair. Two valuable rifles and a Sharp's revolver hung on the wall, and the sash and badge of a scout. I could not help looking at 'Jim' as he stood talking to me. He goes mad with drink at times, swears fearfully, has an ungovernable temper. He has formerly led a desperate life, and is at times even now undoubtedly a ruffian. There is hardly a fireside in Colorado where fearful stories of him as an Indian fighter are not told; mothers frighten their naughty children by telling them that 'Mountain Jim' will get them, and doubtless his faults are glaring, but he is undoubtedly fascinating, and enjoys a popularity or notoriety which no other person has. He offered to be my guide to the plains when I go away. Lyman asked me if I should not be afraid of being murdered, but one could not be safer than with him I have often been told.

The cold was truly awful. I had caught a chill in the morning from putting on my clothes before they were dry, and the warmth of the smoky den was most agreeable; but we had a fearful ride back in the dusk, a gale nearly blowing us off our horses, drifting snow nearly blinding us, and the mercury below zero. I felt as if I were going to be laid up with a severe cold, but the men suggested a trapper's remedy – a tumbler of hot water, with a pinch of cayenne pepper in it – which proved a very rapid cure. They kindly say that if the snow detains me here they also will remain. They tell me that they were horrified when I arrived, as they thought that they could not make me comfortable, and that I had never been used to do anything for myself, and then we complimented each other all round.

THE STORY OF PENGUIN CLASSICS

Before 1946 ...'Classics' are mainly the domain of academics and students, without readable editions for everyone else. This all changes when a little-known classicist, E. V. Rieu, presents Penguin founder Allen Lane with the translation of Homer's *Odyssey* that he has been working on and reading to his wife Nelly in his spare time.

1946 *The Odyssey* becomes the first Penguin Classic published, and promptly sells three million copies. Suddenly, classic books are no longer for the privileged few.

1950s Rieu, now series editor, turns to professional writers for the best modern, readable translations, including Dorothy L. Sayers's *Inferno* and Robert Graves's *The Twelve Caesars*, which revives the salacious original.

1960s The Classics are given the distinctive black jackets that have remained a constant throughout the series's various looks. Rieu retires in 1964, hailing the Penguin Classics list as 'the greatest educative force of the 20th century'.

1970s A new generation of translators arrives to swell the Penguin Classics ranks, and the list grows to encompass more philosophy, religion, science, history and politics.

1980s The Penguin American Library joins the Classics stable, with titles such as *The Last of the Mohicans* safeguarded. Penguin Classics now offers the most comprehensive library of world literature available.

1990s The launch of Penguin Audiobooks brings the classics to a listening audience for the first time, and in 1999 the launch of the Penguin Classics website takes them online to a larger global readership than ever before.

The 21st Century Penguin Classics are rejacketed for the first time in nearly twenty years. This world famous series now consists of more than 1300 titles, making the widest range of the best books ever written available to millions – and constantly redefining the meaning of what makes a 'classic'.

The Odyssey continues ...